eat this with...

Paso Robles Wine

by Lisa Pretty

Paso Robles is full of breathtaking vineyard scenes with oak tree dotted rolling hills. The location I chose for the cover shot was found in the center of Steinbeck Vineyards. The family generously provided me with access to set a table, shoot away and enjoy the peace and beauty of their property.

Pretty Media Creations
179 Niblick Road #102
Paso Robles, CA 93446

ISBN-978-1-61364-633-5

eatthiswith.com

acknowledgements

Producing this book took a huge amount of effort and I couldn't have done it without the help and support of many people.

My friends especially deserve thanks for putting up with my endless talk about food & wine, for helping me test recipes and wine pairings, for bringing new wines to try and for being patient enough to let me photograph every dish before anyone was allowed to eat. With so many palates at my disposal I am sure the recipes and pairings that made it to the book will be enjoyed far more than if I had taste tested on my own.

As word spread that I was working on a Paso Robles food and wine book, the support and contributions were almost overwhelming. The amount of wine and food donated to the project was staggering. Several wineries provided me with a bottle of everything they produced with many others offering a selection of their flagship wines or employee discounts. Friends opened their wine cellars to me, making it possible to experiment with a wide range of wines with every recipe.

With so many people donating food and wine, it is hard to name them all. I would however like to offer a special thank you to Darian Buckles & Will Wooley who provided elk and almost all the beef used to test recipes. Also to Keri Scaggs, who provided the majority of the seafood, all wild caught in Alaska. Having the right ingredients makes all the difference when creating a recipe.

A number of local chefs and foodie friends contributed their favorite recipes. All contributed recipes are noted throughout the book.

Finally I'd like to thank Janis Switzer. Together we have explored new wines for our food & wine columns in the Paso Robles Press. She was kind enough to offer her proof reading skills, catching a large number of my errors, making this book a little easier to read.

contents

Introduction

While you can certainly skip this chapter, it is my way of introducing myself, Paso Robles wines, food & wine pairing and a brief discussion about ingredients.

Read at your leisure or just jump right into making the recipes in this book and experimenting with the many wine pairings. It is hard to go wrong if you are serving Paso Robles wine.

A little about me

Writing this book is something I have thought about for many years. I have enjoyed cooking, experimenting with new recipes and exploring flavor combinations for as long as I can remember. In the early days my "portfolio" of recipes and food experiences were fairly limited. I grew up in Ontario, Canada with a family who enjoyed basic, yet hearty, meals. Roasted chicken, turkey, beef and ham served with potatoes and side vegetables were the traditional Sunday meals. During the week, fish, pork chops, steak, stews and casseroles were typical dishes. With a limited growing season, vegetables were typically canned or frozen.

After leaving home, I became exposed to a much wider range of foods. Herbs, spices and marinades were all very new to me and maybe what inspired me to create my own recipes. Working for a technology company brought me to California where I began my love affair with wine and where I discovered a whole new world of fresh produce.

While living in San Francisco I continued to work in the technology sector as a vice president of international business development. While I hated the airports, constant travel, and long meetings, each place was a new culinary adventure that gave me ideas for recipes. When I could no longer take the constant travel, and really became burnt out on the corporate world, I decided to completely change my life and do something that I enjoyed.

My new life began in Paso Robles, California where I purchased a small winery and shocked everyone by turning into a farmer and making my own wine. I traded in business suits and high heels for jeans and work boots. Instead of flying off to a foreign country my typical travel experience became a drive in a pick-up truck to downtown Paso or perhaps for a real getaway, taking my dog to the coast for a run on the beach. With so much more time spent at home, I had more time to cook, eat and drink wine.

If you are reading this book, chances are very good that you have visited Paso Robles, or at least tried some of the awesome wines from the region. The area has a little bit of everything that makes it the perfect place to live. The weather is terrific all year round (although the locals will sometimes complain if the temperature drops below 30F at night or it rains for 3 days in a row). The people are extremely laid back and friendly. There is a growing base of excellent restaurants. Paso is home to a huge number of vineyards, olive orchards, almond orchards and ranches covered with cattle, sheep and goat. From Paso Robles proper over to the coast there are so many different micro climates that almost every food imaginable can be produced in the area.

So it is here in my office overlooking the estate vineyards, with a happy dog at my side, where I sit and write this book. Paso Robles is not only where I began my career in winemaking, but also where I discovered the impact food can have on wine and vice versa. For many years I had been ordering wine with dinner and gave it only a little thought. More recently I began to research food and wine pairings, really paying attention to how the flavors changed when combined. While working on this book I sometimes tasted up to 12 different wines with food in a day. Throughout this book I am sharing a number of what I consider winning combinations.

Pairing Food and Wine

Some people are very intimidated when it comes to selecting a wine to go with a meal. There really are no rules and when it comes right down to it, if you like the combination it works. While writing this book I spent a little time talking to Chef Jacob at Cass Winery. He didn't have a wine background so I asked if it was hard for him to make the transition from being an executive chef at a restaurant to being a chef at a winery. He said it was really simple, "wine naturally goes with food and in terms of combinations they either work or they don't".

My test to see if a pairing works is to taste the wine on its own, then taste the food, and then re-taste the wine. If the wine tastes as good with the food as it did on its own, then I give it a thumbs up. If the wine tastes even better with the food than it did on its own, I say the pairing has the wow factor. Sometimes the way a food enhances flavors in wine can be surprising…often in a good way…sometimes not.

While there are no hard and fast rules, there are a few things that will help when trying to pair wines. There are some basic characteristics of a wine that will determine which food pairings will work.

Acidity: In general acidity is a good thing. Acidity enhances flavor and in the case of a wine will help it age. The acidity in wine will brighten the flavor of food and will cut through fat. On the other hand, an acidic wine will typically not go well with a creamy dish.

Body: Wines can be light, medium or very full bodied. For the most part you want to pair the body of the wine with the body of the food. For a creamy dish a nice round wine, for a light dish a fairly light, crisp wine. For a juicy steak a big wine usually wins. You get the idea, don't put a delicate white with a spicy rib.

Sweetness: When grapes are fermented the natural sugars in the grapes are converted to alcohol. When almost all of the sugar is converted the wine is considered dry. If some of the sugar is not converted that sugar is referred to as residual sugar. A wine can be off dry as is the case with many Rieslings, to very sweet as is typically found in a Late Harvest Zinfandel. There are times when pairing contrasting levels of sweetness in the food with the sweetness of a wine will work. One thing to be careful of is when it comes to dessert if your dessert is a lot sweeter than your wine it will make your wine seem bitter. Some people say the wine should always be sweeter than the dessert; however, I have found several pairings with the wow factor where that is not the case.

Tannins: While tannins are naturally occurring in wine and soften over time, young wines with lots of tannins will seem very astringent. If you have a tannic wine the best thing to do is serve it with a fatty meat with a bit of spice.

Oak: Oak flavors on both white and red wine can be very pleasant. It will clearly impact the pairing with food. Oaky whites tend to go well with creamy items or roasted foods. Oaky reds are great with grilled food and can hold up to spicy items.

How a food is prepared will also have a lot to do with which wine pairings will work.

Stir-frying: This cooking method is for a fast preparation that preserves the food's flavor and color. Although the type of fat, spice and sauce used will dictate the successful pairings, in general you will want to avoid oaky wines, will want a fairly acidic wine and likely a light to medium bodied wine. White or reds often work here.

Grilling: Grilling uses dry heat and seals all the juices in the meat or vegetable while often leaving a crusty surface. Typically, grilled food will have a smoky flavor making it match well with wines that have a fair amount of oak flavor. In general, full bodied red wines with tannins and bold fruit work well with grilled food. A medium to full bodied white that has been aged in oak can also work well.

Braising and Stewing: The idea of slow cooking in liquid is to soften the meat and provide deep flavors. Typically a fair amount of herbs and spices are used. For braised meats or stews go big. The typical cuts of meat will have some fat that can hold up to tannins and most herbs beg for a bold wine.

A good trick to help a food pair with a wine is to use the wine as part of the cooking process. Create a wine based marinade, use the wine to braise the meat or create a sauce with the wine.

Another tip is the use of herbs, some herbs just naturally pair well with wines. You will find I often use thyme in my recipes. I find thyme enhances

the flavor of almost any red wine.

A final tip is if it is difficult to pair… pick a sparkling wine! There is hardly anything that doesn't pair with Champagne.

Paso Robles Wines

Paso Robles wines have certainly come a long way over the years. Known as the fastest growing wine region in California, Paso has attracted winemakers from all over the world. The soil conditions, hot days and cool evenings make it the ideal growing region and the number of top awards given to wines produced in the area speak to the quality.

What is great about the area is the diversity. The number of different grape varietals that do well in the region is staggering. From the light to the bold, from whites to red, from low to high acidity, you can find almost everything in Paso Robles. There are currently over 200 bonded wineries in the area and over 150 tasting rooms. While the area is widely planted in the well known varietals, you will also find some of the

lesser known varietals planted as well. For a list of the many wines produced in the area see the final chapter in the book "Paso Robles Wines from A to Z". That is also a great place to look for wines to branch out from the pairings I have suggested.

I wish I could say I have tried all of the wines in the A to Z section; however, that is not the case. I included the chapter so if you have a favorite Paso Robles producer or if you have a type of wine you are looking for, you can use that chapter as a reference. I have tasted all of the wines included in the recommended pairings and for my taste the pairings worked well. Taste is very subjective, so find the ones that work for you.

Ingredients

I can't stress enough how important high quality ingredients are when working with a recipe. Just like you cannot make a good wine from bad grapes, you cannot make a gourmet delight without the proper ingredients. Here are a few critical ingredients.

Salt: Almost everything needs a little salt. Salt is a flavor enhancer. Having said that, I tend to go fairly light handed as I like the salt to enhance and not over power. In almost all of my recipes the amount of salt to use will simply be stated as "to taste". I always use high quality, freshly ground sea salt or gourmet salt from some of the finest salt producing areas in the world. I highly recommend tossing the giant shaker of cheap salt and go with a high quality product.

Olive Oil: I use a lot of olive oil, almost always locally produced and extra virgin. A good quality olive oil, especially for drizzling or dipping is essential.

Produce: Unless you live somewhere that it is not available, go fresh with produce. Living in Paso I realize I have it easy since almost everything grows here. I typically have a vegetable and herb garden, most of my friends grow produce, and there is a farmer's market somewhere in the area every day of the week. The trend is to buy locally grown produce and the good thing about that is it also means seasonal. Locally grown, fresh seasonal produce will also be less expensive and higher quality since it is picked at the right time versus ripening in transit.

Fish: If a fish has a strong fish smell, don't purchase it and certainly don't eat it. Fish must be fresh and although there are a few types of fish that are ok farmed, wild caught is the best way to go. I get all of my fish from a reputable source. While working on this book I was lucky enough to have been given a huge quantity of wild-caught salmon from Simply Incredible. The owner was also kind enough to source a wide range of other Alaskan products for me to try. Get to know the people at your local fish market and only buy what is fresh.

Meat: I started eating free range chicken and beef products that are raised without antibiotics and steroids a couple of years ago. What a huge difference in flavor! It may cost more but it is worth it. If you have the freezer space the best thing to do is find a rancher that takes good care of their animals and have it butchered the way you want. The majority of the beef in this book was from a steer named Frank, raised and harvested by my friends at Templeton Hills Beef. They will sell by the full, half or even quarter animal and work with you to have it butchered the way you want. If you don't have the space, get to know your local butcher. Ask questions about where the animal came from, how it was raised and fed. After all it is going into your body. I personally know the families that raised the beef, pork, and goat that I cook with and it is a good feeling.

Hard to find stuff: Some ingredients are a little harder to find but often worth the search. For the most part I have tried to keep the ingredients in this book fairly basic and easy to find. Being very adventurous I couldn't help but to throw in a few that are not as common. I like rabbit, liver, goat and frog legs so have included a recipe for each of those. You may find them frozen at most grocery stores or fresh from a butcher. Other ingredients like pomegranate molasses and Ume plum vinegar, really do make a difference in a recipe. You can typically find those specialty items at a health food store or high end market.

Ok, it is time to get cooking so you can start eating and drinking!

~ ~ ~

Some of my favorite supplers
alcearoseafarm.com
allureestates.com
pier46seafood.com
simplyincredible.com
templetonhillsbeef.com
vivantfinecheese.com
weeolive.com

Nibbles & Bites

When entertaining it is always nice to have something tasty for your guests to nibble on when they arrive. Throughout this chapter you will find a number of recipes that can be made ahead so if you have last minute preparations for the rest of the meal you will not have to worry about hungry guests while you cook.

For casual parties, select several recipes and create a party buffet. All of the nibbles & bites are "finger food", making them ideal for large crowds or times when you just don't want a lot of dirty dishes.

butternut squash dip with blue corn chips - 12
arugula dip with vegetable chips - 13
hummus with pita triangles - 14
olive tapenade crostini - 15
grilled quesadillas - 16
organic tomato and herb flat bread - 17
schiacciata con uva - 18
potato wedges - 19
smoked salmon lettuce petals - 20
red pepper anchovy toasts - 21
smoked salmon cucumber rounds - 22
tilapia ceviche - 23
salmon puffs - 24
chorizo stuffed jalapeños - 25
chicken liver pâté - 26
pork meatballs - 27
15c croquetas de jamon - 28
sausage rolls - 29
blue cheese and caramelized onion sliders - 31

butternut squash dip with blue corn chips

This colorful dip has a little kick. While you can serve it with any chip, the blue corn provides a wonderful color contrast to the bright squash.

1 butternut squash (1 pound)
1 tablespoon olive oil
2 cloves garlic, chopped
2 teaspoons ginger paste
1 teaspoon cayenne pepper
Juice of 1/2 lime
Salt and pepper to taste
1 bag of blue corn chips

- Preheat oven to 375F.

- Place squash on a baking sheet and bake for 40 minutes. Allow squash to cool then cut in half and remove seeds. Scope the flesh from the squash and place in a food processor. Add the remaining ingredients and process until smooth.

- Serve with blue chips and a wedge of lime.

eat this with...

Anglim Syrah
Adelaida Cellars Roussanne
Chumeia Vineyards Chardonnay
DAOU Vineyards Chardonnay
Eos Roussanne
Grey Wolf Roussanne
Jack Creek Cellars Syrah
J. Lohr Chardonnay
Pear Valley Tom's Oak Chardonnay
Penman Springs Syrah
Le Vigne Chardonnay
Rotta Winery Chardonnay

Chapter 2 - Nibbles & Bites

arugula dip with vegetable chips

I make my own beet and sweet potato chips to go with this dip. Just slice the vegetables thin, coat in oil and salt then bake until crisp...or purchase chips already made.

Serves 12

1 cup sour cream
1/4 cup mayonnaise
1 green onion, chopped
2 cups chopped fresh arugula leaves
2 tablespoons chopped fresh basil
Salt, to taste

- Mix all ingredients and place in a food processor. Process until smooth.
- Serve in a dipping bowl with chips or bread on the side.

eat this with...

Caliza Grenache
Derby Pinot Gris
Edward Sellers Grenache Blanc
J Dusi Pinot Gris
Kenneth Volk Roussanne
Meridian Sangiovese
Niner Sangiovese
Still Waters Pinot Gris
Terry Hoage Grenache Blanc

Chapter 2 - Nibbles & Bites

hummus with pita triangles

There are plenty of good hummus options at the store so if you don't have time store bought works well in this situation. I find fresh made always tastes a little better.

Serves 4

14-ounce can of chickpeas, drained
2 cloves of garlic, minced
1 teaspoon cayenne pepper
1 teaspoon cumin
1 tablespoon tahini
3 tablespoons olive oil
Juice of one small lemon
Salt and pepper to taste

- Place all ingredients in a food processor and process until smooth.

- Serve in a bowl with pita triangles on the side. You can dress the hummus up with a drizzle of olive oil, a sprinkle of paprika and toasted pine nuts if desired.

eat this with...

Adelaida Pinot Noir
Anglim Viognier
Bianchi Pinot Grigio
Calcareous Viognier
Caliza Viognier
Halter Ranch Viognier
Hearthstone Pinot Noir
Locatelli Malbec
Maloy O'Neill Pinot Grigio
Nadeau Pinot Grigio
Wild Horse Pinot Noir
Windward Vineyard Pinot Noir

Chapter 2 - Nibbles & Bites

olive tapenade crostini

Here is another one of those oh so very easy to make recipes that people love.

Tapenade
> **1 6-ounce can black olives, drained**
> **1 6-ounce can green olives, drained**
> **2 tablespoons capers**
> **2 cloves garlic chopped**

 Place all ingredients in a food processor and pulse. If mixture appears dry add a drizzle of olive oil and stir.

Crostini
> **1 French baguette**
> **1 tablespoon olive oil**

- Slice bread approximately 1/4 inch.
- Place slices under broiler until they are lightly toasted.
- Flip slices over, brush with oil and return to broiler until golden brown.
- Serve topped olive tapenade or something flavorful.

Note: *Crostinis make great party appetizers. You can top them with goat cheese mixed with herbs, chopped tomatoes with garlic and basil, melted parmesan cheese, smoked salmon with cream cheese...the possibilities are endless. Create a platter with all different toppings including a nice mix of color and textures to pair with a wide range of wine.*

eat this with...
Ancient Peaks Sauvignon Blanc
Bella Luna Sangiovese
Clayhouse Wines Sauvignon Blanc
Chronic Cellars Grenache
Cypher Grenache
Edward Sellars Grenache
Halter Ranch Sauvignon Blanc
J. Lohr Sauvignon Blanc
Niner Wine Sauvignon Blanc
Opolo Sangiovese
Pretty-Smith Palette de Rouge
Zenaida Cellars Grenache

grilled quesadillas

This is one of my "go to" appetizers since they are easy to make, take little time and I usually have the ingredients on hand. Perfect for when friends stop by unexpectedly.

Serves 4
> **2 flour tortillas**
> **3/4 cup grated cheese (your choice or even mixed)**
> **2 tomatoes, pulp removed and chopped**
> **1 green onion, chopped**
> **1 tablespoon chopped fresh basil**
> **1 clove garlic, minced**
> **Hot Sriracha sauce, to taste**
> **Salt to taste**

- Sprinkle cheese on half of each tortilla.
- Mix together remaining ingredients and place on top of cheese.
- Fold tortillas in half and grill over medium heat for 2 minutes per side.
- Let cool for minutes then cut in half. Serve on their own or with guacamole or sour cream.

Note: The recipe above is my basic one for quesadillas. You can create your own with whatever ingredients you have on hand. Goat cheese with tomatoes, green onions and black olives are tasty. Or if you have left over chicken, cube that with lots of cheese and roasted peppers. The type of cheese used and the spice level will really determine which wine pairs best.

eat this with...
Arroyo Robles Zinfandel
Bianchi Sauvignon Blanc
Bodegas M Tempranillo
Castoro Cellars Charbono
Chumeia Zinfandel
Derby Zinfandel
Pear Valley Sauvignon Blanc
Steinbeck Vineyards Zinfandel
Still Waters Sauvignon Blanc
Tobin James Dusi Vineyard Zinfandel

organic tomato and herb flat bread

by Chef Marc LeDuc, Tobin James Cellars

*Pick-up your favorite flat bread and give it a flavor boost with this recipe by Chef Marc.
Great to have on hand for guests to nibble at parties or as a side dish with dinner.*

*Chef Marc recommends using all fresh,
organic herbs in this recipe*

**15 ounces organic tomato sauce
1/2 teaspoon crushed red pepper
1 teaspoon fresh thyme leaves
1 teaspoon fresh oregano
1 teaspoon fresh parsley chopped
1/2 teaspoon minced garlic
1 tablespoon sugar
Salt and pepper, to taste**

- Simmer all ingredients on low heat for 15 minutes and cool for 4 hours

- Spread on your favorite flat bread, and cut into desired serving size pieces

- Garnish with shaved parmesan cheese and fresh chopped herbs (optional)

eat this with...

Tobin James Primo Sangiovese
Tobin James Made in the Shade Merlot
Tobin James Ballistic Zinfandel
Tobin James Rock N Roll Syrah

schiacciata con uva by Maggie D'Ambrosia, Windward Vineyard

This bread is made to celebrate the grape harvest in central Italy. Using the ripe Windward Vineyard estate Pinot Noir grapes, Maggie makes this recipe just once a year during harvest.

Serves 6 - 8

> **1 1/2 pounds Pinot Noir grapes**
> **1/2 cup sugar**
> **1 recipe basic pizza dough,**
>   **risen once**
> **2 tablespoons olive oil**

eat this with...
   Windward Vineyard Estate Pinot Noir

- Remove the grapes from the stems. Wash them well, and pat dry with paper towels. Place in a bowl and sprinkle with the sugar. Set aside until they are needed.

- Knead the dough lightly. Divide it into two halves. Roll out or press one half into a circle about 1/2 inch thick. Place on a lightly oiled flat baking sheet. Sprinkle with half of the sugared grapes.

- Roll out or press the second half of the dough into a circle the same size as the first. Place it on top of the first. Crimp the edges together and sprinkle the top of the remaining grapes. Cover the dough with a dish towel and leave in a warm place to rise for 30 minutes.

- Preheat the oven to 375F.

- Sprinkle the bread with the oil, and bake for 50-60 minutes. Allow to cool before cutting into wedges.

potato wedges

Guys really seem to go for these large roasted potato wedges.

Serves 4
> **2 large russet potatoes**
> **2 tablespoons olive oil**
> **Salt and pepper, to taste**

Dip
> **1/4 cup sour cream**
> **1/4 cup heavy cream**
> **2 tablespoons fresh parsley, chopped**

- Preheat oven to 375F

- Cut the potatoes into large wedges, leaving the skins on. Place wedges on baking sheet, drizzle with olive oil, sprinkle with salt and pepper and toss to coat.

- Roast the potatoes until golden brown, approximately 30 minutes. Turn them after 15-20 minutes.

- Mix together the dip ingredients and serve on the side.

eat this with...

AronHill Primitivo
Calcareous Chardonnay
Caliza Mourvedre
Carmody McKnight Chardonnay
Cypher Mourvedre
Derby Pinot Noir
Lone Madrone Nebbiolo
Pretty-Smith Palette de Rouge
San Marcos Creek Nebbiolo
Tassajara Cellars Pinot Noir
Windward Vineyards Pinot Noir

smoked salmon lettuce petals

Small lettuce petals provide a refreshing base to these tasty appetizers. The fresh pea sprouts really add a nice flavor. If you can't find the sprouts garnish with fresh chopped chives.

Serves 6
- **1/2 pound smoked wild caught salmon**
- **1/4 cup whipped cream cheese**
- **1 tablespoon capers**
- **2 heads of baby romaine lettuce**
- **3/4 cup guacamole**
- **1/4 cup pea sprouts**

- Using a fork, mix together salmon, cream cheese and capers.

- Cut the ends off lettuce and separate into petals.

- Smear each petal with 1/2 tablespoon of guacamole, then layer 1 tablespoon of salmon mixture and garnish with 3-4 pea sprouts.

eat this with...

Cass Winery Rosé
Clavo Cellars Rosé
Clayhouse Chenin Blanc
Chronic Cellars Riesling
DAOU Grenache Blanc
J. Lohr Riesling
Pear Valley Chardonnay
Tablas Creek Grenache Blanc
Tobin James Pink
Wild Horse Malvasia Bianco

Chapter 2 - Nibbles & Bites

red pepper anchovy toasts

Anchovies melted in butter and oil, combined with roasted red peppers and a little cheese is a winning combination. The anchovies do not taste fishy at all when cooked in butter and oil.

Serves 4
>   **1 tablespoon butter**
>   **2 tablespoons olive oil**
>   **1 can anchovy fillets**
>   **2 red bell peppers, roasted, skins**
>   **removed and chopped**
>   **1 tablespoon grated parmesan cheese**
>   **Crusty bread, sliced in thick pieces**

- In a medium sauce pan heat the butter and olive oil. Add the anchovy fillets and stir with a wooden spoon until the anchovies have dissolved.

- Add peppers to the pan and simmer for 10 minutes, stirring occasionally.

- Place bread on a baking sheet, brush the liquid from the pan on bread then place peppers on top. Sprinkle with parmesan cheese and place under broiler until cheese turns golden brown.

eat this with...
Bodegas M Tempranillo
Eberle Sangiovese
Edward Sellers Tempranillo
Epoch Tempranillo
Hearst Ranch Tempranillo
J. Lohr Riesling
Le Vigne Sangiovese
Meridian Riesling
Niner Sangiovese
Pear Valley Rosé
Tobin James Reserve Tempranillo
Villa Creek Tempranillo

smoked salmon cucumber rounds

Cucumbers make a great base for appetizers. Not only do they have a nice fresh flavor but they are also pretty on the platter. I peel half of them for an extra color contrast.

Serves 8

2 cups flaked smoked salmon
1/4 cup whipped cream cheese
2 tablespoons fresh dill, chopped
1 long English cucumber, sliced
2 tablespoons capers

- Mix together salmon, cheese and dill.
- Place cucumber rounds on a platter. Place a spoonful of the salmon mixture on each round.
- Place one caper on each round and sprinkle any remaining capers on the platter.
- Serve chilled

eat this with...

Castoro Cellars Gewurztraminer
Clayhosue Chenin Blanc
Eos Pinot Blanc
J Dusi Pinot Gris
J&J Cellars Sparkling
JUSTIN Sauvignon Blanc
Le Vigne Sparkling
Meridian Riesling
Mitchella Sauvignon Blanc
Pear Valley Sauvignon Blanc

Chapter 2 - Nibbles & Bites

tilapia ceviche

The acid of the lime juice cooks the fish and provides a wonderful texture. This may be my all time favorite appetizer. Serve with chips, crackers or Belgium endive petals.

Serves 6

2 tilapia fillets, diced
Juice of 3-4 fresh limes
6 cherry tomatoes, diced
1 green onion diced
1 clove garlic, minced
1/2 teaspoon hot chili sauce
2 tablespoons fresh cilantro, chopped
Salt & pepper, to taste

- Place the fish in a glass container with a tight fitting lid. Pour lime juice over fish, stirring to coat all fish pieces. If fish pieces are not covered completely, add more lime juice. Cover and refrigerate for 3 hours.

- Drain and discard lime juice. Mix the fish with the remaining ingredients.

- Serve chilled.

eat this with...

Bodegas M Albarniño
Bodegas Paso Robles Albarniño
Edward Sellers Grenache Blanc
Grey Wolf Grenache Blanc
Halter Ranch Sauvignon Blanc
J. Lohr Chardonnay
Le Vigne Chardonnay
Lone Madrone Albarniño
Opolo Chardonnay
Pear Valley Chardonnay
Silver Horse Albarniño
Tablas Creek Picpoul Blanc

Chapter 2 - Nibbles & Bites

salmon puffs

These salmon puffs can be made with canned salmon or flaked smoked salmon. If you make them in a larger turnover format they can be served as a small plate or brunch item.

18 puffs

    2 7-ounce cans salmon, drained
    1/4 cup cream cheese
    2 green onions chopped
    1 package puff pastry sheets, thawed
    1 egg, beaten
    1 tablespoon water

eat this with...

Ancient Peaks Sauvignon Blanc
Cass Winery Sparkling
J&J Cellars Sparkling
JUSTIN Sauvignon Blanc
Hearst Ranch Sauvignon Blanc
Eberle Sauvignon Blanc
Meridian Gewurztraminer
Niner Sauvignon Blanc
Pear Valley Sauvignon Blanc
Riverstar Sauvignon Blanc
Still Waters Sauvignon Blanc
Treana White

- Preheat oven to 400F.

- Combine salmon, cheese and onions.

- Cut each puff pastry sheet into 9 rectangles. Place a spoonful of salmon mixture in the center of each rectangle.

- Mix egg and water together. Brush egg mixture along the edges of each rectangle. Fold the rectangle in half and use a fork to press edges together. Pierce each rectangle in the center with the fork. Brush the top of each pastry with egg mixture.

- Bake in oven until pastry puffs and turns golden brown, approximately 15 minutes.

- Cut in half for bite size pieces and serve warm or at room temperature.

Chapter 2 - Nibbles & Bites

chorizo stuffed jalapeños

These spicy little bites will add a little life to any get together.

12 pieces
> 1 tablespoon olive oil
> 1/4 pound chorizo
> Salt & pepper to taste
> 6 jalapeño peppers, cut in half and seeded
> 1/4 cup crumbled feta cheese

- Heat oil in a small frying pan. Sauté chorizo seasoned with salt and pepper at high heat until it is cooked through, approximately 15 minutes.

- Place chorizo in pepper halves and top with feta crumbles.

- Place under broiler until cheese begins to brown.

eat this with...
Carmody McKnight Sparkling
Clavo Cellars Sauvignon Blanc
Derby Pinot Gris
Eberle Pinot Grigio
J Dusi Pinot Gris
J&J Cellars Sparkling
Hearst Ranch Sauvignon Blanc
Le Vigne Pinot Grigio
Opolo Pinto Grigio
San Marcos Creek Sauvignon Blanc
Still Waters Pinot Gris
Tobin James Sauvignon Blanc

chicken liver pâté

Chicken liver is inexpensive and when combined with brandy produces a nice pâté . Serve on crispy crackers or bread.

1/2 +1/4 cup unsalted butter
1 cup finely chopped onion
1/4 teaspoon dried thyme
1/4 teaspoon dried marjoram
1/4 teaspoon dried sage
Salt & pepper, to taste
1 pound chicken livers, trimmed
2 tablespoons brandy

eat this with...

Ancient Peaks Rosé
Calcareous Rosé
Cass Winery Rosé
Edward Sellers Rosé
Graveyard Paso Thombstone Pink
Halter Ranch Rosé
Pear Valley Rosé
Penman Springs Two Roses Rosé
Tobin James Pink

- Melt 1/2 cup (1 stick) butter in a large frying pan over medium heat, then sauté onion and garlic for 5 minutes. Add herbs, salt, pepper and livers and cook, stirring, until livers are cooked outside but still pink when cut open, about 8 minutes. Stir in brandy and cook for 3 more minutes. Purée mixture in a food processor until smooth, then transfer pâté to a large ramekin and smooth the top.

- Melt remaining 1/4 cup (1/2 stick) butter in small saucepan over low heat, then remove pan from heat and let butter stand 3 minutes. Skim froth from butter, then spoon enough clarified butter over pâté to cover its surface, leaving milky solids in bottom of pan.

- Chill pâté until butter is firm, about 30 minutes, then cover with plastic wrap and chill at least 2 hours longer. The pâté can be stored with butter coating in the refrigerator for up to 2 weeks. Once butter seal is broken eat within one week.

Chapter 2 - Nibbles & Bites

pork meatballs

Meatballs can be dressed up for a fancy party. These pork based meatballs have a little spice and when drizzled with sauce and placed on appetizer toothpicks they actually look elegant.

Meatballs
- 1/2 pound ground pork
- 1 egg
- 1 clove garlic, minced
- 2 tablespoons finely chopped onion
- 1/4 cup bread crumbs
- 1/4 teaspoon dried thyme
- 1 teaspoon ground paprika
- 1 teaspoon cayenne pepper
- Salt, to taste
- 1/4 cup olive oil
- Flour for dusting

Sauce
- 2 garlic cloves, minced
- 1/2 yellow bell pepper, chopped
- 1/2 orange bell pepper, chopped
- 1 teaspoon dried chili flakes
- 3/4 cup chicken broth

- Combine ground pork, egg, garlic, onion, bread crumbs, thyme, paprika, pepper and salt. Form into teaspoon-size balls (you should have about 20). Heat oil in a medium frying pan. Dust meatballs with flour and brown evenly on all sides in hot oil. Remove from oil and place on paper towels to remove any oil.

- Sauté garlic, onion and peppers in the hot oil. Add chili flakes and chicken broth and cook 10 minutes. Add meatballs to sauce and cook for 10 minutes longer, turning often until sauce thickens and meatballs are cooked through.

- Place meatballs on serving plate with sauce spooned over top and insert a toothpick in each meatball. Serve warm.

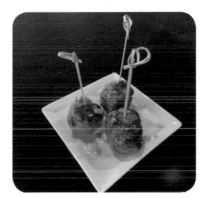

eat this with...
Anglim Marsanne
Bodegas Paso Robles Albariño
Austin Hope Grenache
Caliza Grenache
Edward Sellers Grenache
San Marcos Creek Nebbiolo
Silver Horse Albariño

15c croquetas de jamon by Ali Rush Carscaden

15c is a wine shop and bar in Templeton that offers over 500 wines from around the world and specializes is small local producers. Every Thursday they offer a Spanish Tapas bar and cook up all sorts of traditional small bites that pair well with their wines. The croquetas are one of their signature favorites and pairs very well with wine. Ali recommends a Rhône like Vermentino or for the red fans, try a fruity Grenache.

18 croquetas

- 2 tablespoons butter
- 3/4 cup flour
- 1 1/2 cups cream
- 1/2 teaspoon nutmeg
- Dash of ground pepper & salt
- 1/2 cup very finely diced chorizo bilbao
- 2 eggs, lightly beaten with 2 teaspoons water
- Panko bread crumbs for coating
- Safflower olive oil for frying
- ¾ cup diced manchego cheese

- In large pan melt butter and fry up the diced chorizo.

- Add flour and stir to soak up the grease.

- Sprinkle in salt, pepper and nutmeg.

- Pour in cream and stir until thick paste forms.

- Transfer mixture into a bowl and chill for 2 hours.

- Add diced manchego and mix.

- Roll dough into balls (golf ball size).

- Roll each ball in flour, then egg mixture, then bread crumbs.

- Fry until golden brown and serve immediately with Roasted Pepper Aoili.

Roasted Pepper Aoili

- 4 red peppers
- Egg yolk
- Garlic clove
- Salt & pepper
- Olive oil

- Roast red peppers in the broiler until skin is brown.
- Let peppers cool and peel off skin.
- In blender, mix pepper, egg yolk, garlic clove and a pinch of salt and pepper.
- Slowly pour in olive oil until desired texture (about ¼ cup of oil).
- Serve in a small dipping bowl with croquetas.

eat this with...

Clavo Vermentino
Edward Sellers Grenache
Hearst Ranch Tempranillo
Lone Madrone Le Mezcla
Silver Horse Tempranillo
Tablas Creek Vermentino
Villa Creek Grenache

sausage rolls by Steve Kroener, Silver Horse

These sausage rolls are easy to make with pre-made dough. Bake up a bunch for your next party.

Makes 20 portions
- **1 package Pillsbury Crescent Rolls**
- **1 pound of your favorite sausage (uncooked)**

- Preheat oven to 375F.

- On a floured surface unwrap the dough and keep together in a large rectangle.

- Spread uncooked sausage over the dough and completely cover. Sausage should be about a 1/4 thick.

- Roll up the sausage and the dough layers lengthwise to make a log. Wrap the log in foil and place in fridge for 30 minutes to harden up.

- Remove from fridge and unwrap log. Cut log into 1/2 inch slices. Place on cookie sheet and bake till golden brown about 15 minutes.

- Remove from oven and let cool 2 minutes then serve.

eat this with...
Silver Horse Tomori

         Chapter 2 - Nibbles & Bites

blue cheese and caramelized onion sliders

They may be little in size but they are big in flavor. Be sure to use high quality lean ground beef.

Makes 12 sliders
- **2 medium sweet onions, thinly sliced**
- **1/4 cup salted butter**
- **1 teaspoon dried sage**
- **1 pound lean ground beef**
- **3 ounces gorgonzola crumbles**
- **1 egg, beaten**
- **2 tablespoons Worcestershire sauce**
- **Salt & pepper to taste**
- **12 mini buns**

- Melt butter in medium sauce pan over medium heat. Stir in sliced onions and sage. Reduce heat to simmer. Simmer onions until they caramelize (approximately 3 hours), stirring occasionally. The onions may be prepared the day before. If prepared in advance, refrigerate in a sealed container and reheat prior to inserting in bun.

- Mix beef, cheese, egg, Worcestershire sauce, salt and pepper together until well combined. Form into 12 small patties. Grill patties on medium heat for approximately 2 minutes per side.

- Place grilled patties inside bun with a generous portion of caramelized onions.

eat this with...

Ancient Peaks Zinfandel
Candor Zinfandel
Liberty School Cabernet Sauvignon
Pear Valley Syrah
Penman Springs Syrah
Pretty-Smith Cabernet Sauvignon
Riverstar Syrah
Starr Ranch Syrah
Still Waters Syrah
Tobin James Silver Reserve Syrah
Troublemaker

Small Plates

The small plate recipes in this chapter can be served as an appetizer, a lunch plate, or select several to create a full dinner menu. I often order a few appetizer items from a menu in a restaurant so I can experience a wider selection of flavors in small portions. Why not do the same when entertaining at home?

eggplant roll-ups - 34
polenta rounds - 35
portabella mushroom ciabatta roll -36
wild mushroom and goat cheese tart -37
grilled portabella mushrooms - 38
stuffed tomatoes - 39
pizza - 40
smoked salmoncakes - 42
spicy crabcakes - 43
low country shrimp & grits - 45
mussels & chorizo - 46
smoked scallops wrapped in prosciutto - 47
grilled shrimp - 49
mediterranean calamari steak - 51
shrimp rolls - 53
chorizo stuffed peppers - 55
thai satay - 57
chicken vol au vent - 58
sautéed frog legs - 59
petite top sirloin burgers - 61
eggplant towers - 62

eggplant roll-ups by Pat & Pete Lareau, travel-and-eat.blogspot.com

These eggplant roll-ups make a very tasty and attractive small plate.

Serves 4-6

1 eggplant
1/3 cup soft fresh goat cheese
10 sprigs of dill
2 tablespoons pine nuts, toasted
2 tablespoons olive oil
Juice of 1/2 lemon (1 tablespoon)
¼ teaspoon grated lemon zest
Ground black pepper

eat this with...

Calcareous Chardonnay
Eberle Sangiovese
J&J Cellars Sparkling
Le Vigne Sparkling
Pretty-Smith Cabernet Franc
Niner Sangiovese
Peachy Canyon Sangiovese
Ranchita Canyon Sangiovese
San Marcos Creek White Merlot
Tobin James Sangiovese

- Use a mandolin to thinly slice (1/4") the peeled eggplant. Keep the 10 best slices.

- Lay slices out on paper towel and salt. After 15 minutes, press with another paper towel to soak up bitter liquid. Turn and repeat for second side.

- Spray eggplant lightly with olive oil and grill over hot coals or hot gas grill briefly. Be watchful and turn, they can burn easily.

- Spread each eggplant slice with room temperature goat cheese. Sprinkle with toasted pine nuts. Put one sprig of dill across the middle of each slice so that it shows out the side. Roll up along the lengthwise and place seam side down on a plate.

- Just before serving, drizzle with dressing made from 1 part lemon juice, 2 parts olive oil, pepper and grated lemon zest

polenta rounds

You can always make your own polenta and form rounds. This is one time I like to save time by purchasing the polenta pre made in a tube format.

Serves 6

1 tube pre made polenta
1+1 tablespoon olive oil
1 red pepper chopped
1 clove garlic, minced
1 small red onion, chopped
1 small zucchini, chopped
1/2 cup chopped mushrooms
2 teaspoons dried thyme
Salt and pepper, to taste
1/4 cup crumbled feta cheese

- Preheat oven to 400F.

- Cut polenta into rounds 1/4 inch thick and brush both sides with olive oil. Place on a baking sheet and bake for 10 minutes. Turn rounds over after 5 minutes.

- Heat olive oil in a large frying pan, sauté pepper, garlic, onion, zucchini and mushrooms for 5 minutes. Add thyme, salt and pepper and sauté for an additional 5 minutes. Turn heat off and stir in feta cheese.

- Spoon vegetable mixture on top of polenta rounds and bake for 5 minutes.

eat this with...
Ancient Peaks Merlot
Carmody McKnight Cabernet Franc
Derby Cabernet Franc
Hearst Ranch Merlot
Pretty-Smith Cabernet Franc
Vina Robles Red [4]

portabella mushroom ciabatta roll

This recipe can be served as a small plate when made with a warm ciabatta roll, or place the mushroom mixture on a toasted crostini to serve as finger food at a party.

Serves 4

> **1 tablespoon olive oil**
> **1 clove garlic, minced**
> **1 small onion, sliced and halved**
> **4 medium baby portabella mushrooms, sliced**
> **1 tablespoon dried thyme**
> **Salt & pepper to taste**
> **1/2 cup dry red wine**
> **1 tablespoon Worcestershire sauce**
> **1/2 roasted red bell pepper, diced**
> **2 ciabatta rolls**
> **4 tablespoons parmesan cheese, shaved (optional)**
> **Fresh thyme or basil (optional)**

- Preheat oven to 350F

- Heat oil in large frying pan. Sauté garlic and onions until onions begin to soften then add mushrooms. Continue to sauté until mushrooms begin to release their juice. Add thyme, salt, pepper, wine and Worcestershire sauce. Stir and bring to a boil. Reduce heat to simmer for 5 minutes, add pepper and simmer for an additional 5 minutes.

- After adding peppers place rolls in oven to warm for 5 minutes.

- Slice rolls in half horizontally and place on plates, top with mushroom mixture and garnish with cheese and/or fresh herbs if desired.

eat this with...

AronHill Cabernet Sauvignon
Caliza Cabernet Sauvignon
Cass Winery Cabernet Sauvignon
Chateau Margene Cabernet Sauvignon
Clayhouse Cabernet Sauvignon
Denner Syrah
Jack Creek Cellars Syrah
JUSTIN Cabernet Sauvignon
Graveyard Cabernet Sauvignon
Pomar Junction Syrah
Wild Horse Unbridled Pinot Noir
Windward Vineyard Pinot Noir

Chapter 3 - Small Plates

wild mushroom and goat cheese tart

Be sure to use high quality, fresh goat cheese in these tarts. The pastry, cheese and mushrooms combine to make a lovely appetizer.

Serves 6

6 Phyllo sheets
1/4 cup unsalted butter, melted
1 tablespoon olive oil
2 cups wild mushrooms, chopped
Salt and pepper to taste
1/4 teaspoon dried thyme
1/4 teaspoon ground sage
3 ounces fresh goat cheese
1 tablespoon chopped chives
1 tablespoon pine nuts, toasted
1 tablespoon fresh chopped herbs

- Preheat oven to 400F. Cut phyllo sheets into squares large enough to cover the base of a muffin tin with the edges overlapping on top. Layer six squares in each muffin slot, brushing butter on each square as you go. The squares should be offset from one another to form a pretty pattern. Bake for 15 minutes to form the base for the tarts.
- Heat oil in a medium sized pan and sauté the mushrooms. You can use any type of mushrooms, I like to mix oyster, shitake and morels. When mushrooms begin to release their juices, add salt, pepper, thyme and sage. Continue to sauté until mushrooms are soft (approximately 5 minutes.
- Mix together goat cheese and chives. Place goat cheese on the base of each tart shell. Place mushrooms on top of the goat cheese then garnish with pine nuts and herbs.

eat this with...

Adelaida Cellars Pinot Noir
Anglim Pinot Noir
Calcareous Pinot Noir
Tablas Creek Roussanne
Wild Horse Unbridled Pinot Noir
Windward Vineyard Pinot Noir

grilled portabella mushrooms

Really large portabella mushrooms are perfect for grilling. With all the space inside the cap they are fun to stuff. This recipe is a healthy alternative to pizza.

Serves 2

3 cloves garlic, finely chopped
2 tablespoons olive oil
1 teaspoon dried thyme
1 tablespoon soy sauce
1 tablespoon balsamic vinegar
2 large portabella mushrooms, stems removed
1 roasted red bell pepper, skin removed, chopped
4 ounces fresh mozzarella, sliced
1/4 cup fresh basil, chopped

eat this with...

Caliza Tempranillo
Cass Rosé
Eberle Sangiovese
Le Vigne Sangiovese
Mission View Padre's Choice
Niner Sangiovese
Pretty-Smith Cabernet Sauvignon
Tobin James Tempranillo

- In a small bowl mix together garlic, oil, thyme, soy sauce and vinegar.

- Pour mixture into the mushroom caps and allow to marinate for 30 minutes.

- Place mushrooms on grill at medium heat. Grill mushrooms for 15 minutes.

- Place pepper, mozzarella and basil on mushrooms and grill for an additional 5 minutes.

stuffed tomatoes

Make plenty of these since everyone always seem to want seconds. Be sure to use fresh, ripe tomatoes that are bursting with color and flavor.

Serves 6 (or 4 as a lunch)

1 can white tuna, drained
1 can white beans, drained and rinsed
1 green onion, finely chopped
3 medium basil leaves, chopped
Juice of one lemon
Salt and pepper to taste
12 medium tomatoes

- In a medium bowl, mix together tuna, beans, onion and basil (reserve a small amount of basil for garnish). Squeeze lemon juice over mixture, sprinkle with salt and pepper and stir.

- Cover the bowl and set in the refrigerator for at least one hour to let the flavors combine.

- Wash tomatoes then cut the top off and scoop seeds/pulp from each tomato's core

- Spoon the stuffing into the tomato shells and garnish with basil. Serve three per plate on a bed of greens for a lunch entrée or two per plate as an appetizer.

eat this with...

DAOU Viognier
Eberle Côte-du-Rôbles Blanc
Kenneth Volk Roussanne
Opolo Roussanne
Pear Valley Chardonnay
Tablas Creek Picpoul Blanc
Tobin James Chardonnay
Wild Horse Verdelho

pizza by Steve Kroener, Silver Horse

At Silver Horse the wood burning pizza oven is loaded with wood so pizzas can be made on a regular basis. You don't have to have a pizza oven to try Steve's recipes at home!

Pizza Dough - yields 4-5 10 inch pizzas

1 ½ - cups warm water
1 teaspoon active dry yeast
4 cups superfine flour
1 teaspoon salt
1 teaspoon sugar
1 teaspoon olive oil

- Place ¼ cup of warm water in a small bowl and slowly stir in the yeast. Let sit for 5 minutes or until yeast is creamy.

- Place flour, salt, sugar, yeast mixture and remaining water into a mixer bowl. Add dough hook to mixer. Mix on low for 2 minutes. If after 2 minutes, dough looks too wet and sticky add 1 flour tablespoon at a time while mixing till dough looks shaggy. Drizzle oil and mix for 2 more minutes. Dough should form a smooth ball and clear the side of the bowl. Turn mixer off, cover bowl with plastic wrap, and let rest for 20 minutes. Remove plastic wrap and mix the dough for an addition 3 minutes until dough forms a smooth ball and clears the side of the bowl. Remove dough from mixing bowl and place in a lightly oiled bowl and cover with plastic wrap. Let sit at room temperature for 2 ½ hours or until doubled in size.

- Once doubled in size, pre-heat your oven to 500F or turn on your grill to high. If using a pizza stone place in oven or on grill at this time. Then lightly flour counter top and place dough ball on top of floured surface. Roll the dough out into a log and section into 4 or 5 pieces. Set aside and add another dusting of flour to your counter top. One at a time flatten out dough piece by hand or with a rolling pin. Do not worry about a perfectly round pizza. These are hand-made and should look as such. Pizza should be at least ¼ inch thick.

- If baking in the oven place pizza dough on a floured baking sheet. Add pizza toppings and slide pizza into the oven's middle rack or slide pizza directly onto the grill. If using a pizza stone, slide pizza onto stone. Close the oven door or grill lid and monitor every three minutes. Once the pizza dough is golden brown remove from heat and let stand for a few minutes to cool and cut.

Chapter 3 - Small Plates

pizza margherita 1 serving
(multiply by number of pizzas desired)

**1 cup good quality tomatoes, undrained,
crushed or coarsely chopped.
1/4 cup basil leaves
2 ounces fresh mozzarella cheese, sliced
Pinch black pepper
Extra virgin olive oil**

❧ Place pizza on baking sheet. Starting at the center of the dough, spoon on the tomatoes and with the backside of the spoon and spread out in a circular motion, keeping 1 inch around the outer edge. Tear the basil leaves and scatter around the pizza. Top with the fresh mozzarella, sprinkle the black pepper, and drizzle with oil. Place in the oven.

at this with...
Silver Horse The Big Easy

eat this with...
Silver Horse Tempranillo

pizza bianco 1 serving
(multiply by number of pizzas desired)

**2 tablespoons extra virgin olive oil
1 medium sweet yellow onion
1 teaspoon fresh chopped thyme
2 tablespoons crumbled blue cheese
Pinch of salt
Pinch of black pepper**

❧ Heat olive oil in a small pan over low heat. Add onions and salt and cook slowly for 45 minutes or until caramelized. Stir occasionally and do not adjust heat. We do not want to fry the onions! Remove the mixture from the heat and add thyme. Spread mixture over the pizza dough, top with blue cheese, and sprinkle with black pepper. Place in oven.

smoked salmoncakes

Not only do these make a nice small plate, but they are also great leftover for breakfast or brunch.

eat this with...

Chumeia Chardonnay
Clayhouse Chenin Blanc
Cypher Winery Chardonnay
Graveyard Paso Tombstone White
J&J Cellars Sparkling
Pear Valley Our Daily White
Tassajara Cellars Chardonnay

Serves 4

4 russet potatoes, peeled and cut in 2-inch cubes
1+3 tablespoons olive oil
1 large onion, chopped
1 large egg, beaten
1/2 pound smoked salmon, chopped
3/4 cup Panko bread crumbs
Salt & pepper to taste

Cream Topping

1/2 cup sour cream
1/2 cup heavy cream
2 tablespoons fresh chives, chopped

- Stir together sour and heavy cream

- Boil potatoes in salted water until soft, approximately 15 minutes. Drain and mash.

- In a large frying pan, heat 1 tablespoon of oil and saute onions until soft. Add onion, egg, and salmon to mashed potatoes. Season with salt and pepper to taste, stir until well combined, then form into cakes and lightly coat with bread crumbs.

- Heat the remaining oil in the frying pan and fry salmon cakes approximately 2 minutes per side. They should be golden brown.

- Serve with a dollop of cream and garnish with chives.

Chapter 3 - Small Plates

spicy crabcakes by John Teeling, Calcareous Vineyard

Everyone loves a good crabcake. Try this recipe by John Teeling with his basil orange aioli and a glass of Calcareous' Viognier/Marsanne blend.

Crabcakes

- 1 pound crab meat
- ¾ cup bread crumbs
- 3 tablespoons cream
- 3 tablespoons mayonnaise
- 1 egg
- ¼ cup chopped parsley
- 1/8 cup chopped red onion
- ½ teaspoon kosher salt
- ¼ teaspoon white pepper
- ¼ teaspoon black pepper
- ¼ tcaspoon red pepper flakes

- Mix all ingredients together by hand and mold into cakes.
- Sauté in oil till golden.
- Serve with Basil Orange Aioli.

Basil Orange Aioli

- 3 ounces frozen orange juice concentrate
- 1 cup mayonnaise
- 2 tablespoons chopped garlic
- 1 cup packed fresh basil leaves

eat this with...
Calcareous Viognier/Marsanne

- Combine ingredients in food processor and blend until smooth.

low country shrimp & grits by Chef Debi Loftis, Haven Wine Bistro

Haven Wine Bistro, in Atascadero, offers a huge selection of Paso Robles wines by the taste, glass or bottle. Most Thursday evenings Haven will feature a local winemaker and Chef Debi will pair four dishes with four wines from the featured winery. Her creations are always delicious and often have a little twist to show her southern roots. Try her low country shrimp and grits recipe at home with a glass of rosé.

Serves 4

1 1/2 pounds andouille sausage, sliced on the bias
1/2 cup canola oil
1/2 cup green peppers, julienned
1/2 cup poblano peppers, julienned
2 cups onions, julienned
8 teaspoons blackening spice
4 tablespoons corn
8 tablespoons tomatoes, diced
3 teaspoons salt
4 teaspoons garlic, chopped
2 pounds shrimp (16-20 ct)
4 teaspoons green onion, sliced

4 teaspoons Italian parsley, chopped
4 teaspoons parmesan cheese
40 ounces stone ground grits
1 cup white wine
4 cups heavy cream

Blackening Spice

2-1/2 tablespoons smoked paprika
2 tablespoons salt
2 tablespoons garlic powder
1-1/4 tablespoon freshly ground black pepper
1 tablespoon onion powder
1- 1/4 tablespoon cayenne
1 tablespoon dried oregano
1 tablespoon dried thyme

- Prepare grits following package directions (be sure to use stone ground and not instant).
- Sauté andouille sausage until browned and set aside.
- In oil, sauté onions and peppers over medium heat for 3 minutes Add vegetables, spices, shrimp, parmesan and andouille and continue to sauté for 4 minutes.
- Add wine and reduce for 5 minutes.
- Add heavy cream and reduce for 3 minutes or until thickened.
- Place grits in the bottom of the bowl, top with shrimp mixture and garnish with parsley and parmesan prior to serving.

eat this with...

Caliza Rosé
Denner Theresa
Epoch Rosé
Halter Ranch Rosé
J. Lohr Rosé
Penman Springs Rosé

mussels & chorizo by Pat & Pete Lareau, travel-and-eat.blogspot.com

This Spanish small plate dish can be served in larger portions as an entree.

Serves 6

1/4 cup extra-virgin olive oil
½ pound dry cured Spanish chorizo, finely chopped
3 shallots, finely chopped
1 tablespoon minced garlic
1/2 cup dry white wine
4 pounds mussels, cleaned
16 ounces clam juice
1/4 cup finely chopped fresh flat-leaf parsley
1/2 cup finely chopped fresh cilantro
2 tablespoons fresh lemon juice

eat this with...

Bodegas Paso Robles Viva Yo
Edward Sellers Grenache
Silver Horse Tempranillo
Halter Ranch Grenache
Hearst Ranch Malbec
Mitchella Grenache
Tobin James Primitivo
Villa Creek Grenache

- Heat oil in a 12-inch heavy skillet over moderately high heat until hot but not smoking, then sauté chorizo and shallots, stirring, until chorizo is golden brown on edges, about 4 minutes. Add garlic and sauté, stirring, 1 minute. Add wine and simmer until liquid is reduced by half, about 5 minutes. Keep sauce warm, covered. (Can also do this ahead and reheat at last minute).

- Steam the mussels in clam juice in a large covered pot. This should be done just before serving. Reserve the hot liquid.

- Place the mussels in 4 bowls and add the hot liquid to the chorizo mixture (take care not to pour the sediment as it might contain sand). Add the lemon juice and parsley to the liquid and then pour over the bowls of mussels. Sprinkle liberally with the cilantro. Serve with lots of crusty country bread for dipping.

smoked scallops wrapped in prosciutto

If you like to smoke fish and meat try a batch of large sea scallops. I source mine already smoked. While they are delicious cold, when placed under the broiler the flavors really come together.

Serves 6

6 5-inch long fresh rosemary sprigs
12 large smoked sea scallops
3 ounces prosciutto, thinly sliced

- Pull the leaves off the bottom three inches of each rosemary sprig and soak in water for 20 minutes.

- Wrap each scallop in prosciutto. Using rosemary as skewers, place two wrapped scallops per skewer.

- Place skewers on a baking sheet and broil for 1 minute per side. The rosemary and prosciutto flavors will be absorbed in the flesh of the smoked scallops.

eat this with...

Caliza Viognier
DAOU Viognier
Eberle Côtes-du-Rôbles Blanc
Edward Sellers Viognier
Grey Wolf Viognier
Pear Valley Our Daily White
Robert Hall Viognier
Steinbeck Vineyards Viognier
Tablas Creek Côtes de Tables Blanc
Vina Robles White [4]

grilled shrimp

Marinated, grilled and served with a spicy sauce for dipping. How could anyone not like these served on a skewer. Pick your favorite sauce...or make both!

Serves 4

1 pound of large shrimp, peeled and deveined (leave tails on)

Marinade

2 cloves garlic, smashed and chopped
Juice of 1 lime
1 teaspoon cayenne pepper
2 tablespoons olive oil
1/2 cup dry white wine

- Place shrimp in zip lock bag. Mix together marinade and pour over shrimp, shake to coat, seal bag and marinate for 20 minutes. While the shrimp are marinating, if you are using wooden skewers, soak them in water.
- Place shrimp on skewers and grill (approximately 2 minutes per side). Be sure not to over cook.
- Serve sauce on the side for dipping.

Garlic Sauce

3 tablespoons olive oil
4 large cloves of garlic, finely minced
1 teaspoon sweet Spanish paprika
1 teaspoon red pepper flakes
1/4 cup dry sherry
2 tablespoons chopped fresh parsley

- Heat oil in pan and sauté garlic until it begins to brown. Add paprika, pepper and sherry. Simmer for 15 minutes -- just before serving, stir in fresh parsley.

Curry Sauce

1 tablespoon olive oil
1 onion, chopped
1 clove of garlic, chopped
1 cup "Thick" coconut milk
1 tablespoon hot curry powder (adjust to taste)
1/2 tablespoon brown sugar
2 teaspoons cayenne pepper
1/4 cup crushed roasted peanuts
2 tablespoons fresh chopped basil

- Heat oil in pan, sauté onion and garlic. Add coconut milk, curry, cayenne pepper, brown sugar and nuts. Heat curry sauce over medium heat, stirring frequently. Once sauce comes to a boil reduce heat and simmer for 15 minutes -- just before serving stir in fresh chopped basil.

eat this with...

Bodegas Paso Robles Doña Blanca
Bodegas Paso Robes Galicia
Castoro Cellars Gewurztraminer
Eos Gewurztraminer
Kenneth Volk Verdelho
Silver Horse Albariño
Wild Horse Verdelho

mediterranean calamari steak

For a very inexpensive piece of fish, calamari steak can be made into a very impressive appetizer. Be careful not to overcook the calamari since it can become tough when overdone.

Serves 4

2 tablespoons olive oil
1 shallot, finely chopped
2 cloves of garlic, finely chopped
1 red bell pepper, cut into strips
1 medium yellow summer squash,
    cut into half moons
1 medium zucchini, cut into half moons
½ cup sliced black olives
½ cup of dry white wine or vegetable stock

4 medium sized tomatoes, blanched,
    peeled and coarsely chopped
1 teaspoon cayenne pepper
1 teaspoon dried thyme
Salt to taste
2 calamari steaks, cut into strips
½ cup feta cheese
2 tablespoons fresh parsley, chopped

- Heat olive oil and sauté shallot and garlic until they just begin to brown, add red pepper strips and continue to sauté for 5 minutes then add squash and sauté for an additional 2-3 minutes.

- Stir in olives, wine, tomatoes, pepper, thyme and salt. Bring to a boil and then reduce heat to simmer.

- In a frying pan, heat olive oil and sauté calamari strips for one minute, then add to simmering pot. Simmer for 1 additional minute. Take care not to over cook the calamari as it will become very tough.

- Divide into bowls, crumble feta cheese into each bowl and garnish with parsley.

eat this with...

Derby Pinot Noir
Jack Creek Cellars Pinot Noir
J. Lohr Pinto Noir
Kenneth Volk Pinot Noir
Le Vigne Pinot Noir
Tassajara Cellars Pinot Noir
Tobin James Pinot Envy
Venteux Pinot Noir
Wild Horse Cheval Sauvage Pinot Noir
Windward Vineyard Pinot Noir

shrimp rolls

Rice paper is very easy to work with. You can roll almost anything in rice paper to create an impressive appetizer. Don't forget the sauce for dipping!

Serves 4

4 large round rice paper wrappers
1 cup shrimp, deveined, peeled and cooked
Juice of 1 lemon
1/4 cup chopped fresh basil
1/2 cup spicy sprouts
1/2 cup chopped mixed greens
1 avocado, chopped
1/2 cucumber, peeled and chopped
1 tablespoon sesame oil
Hot Sriracha sauce, to taste

Dipping Sauce

2 tablespoons soy sauce
2 teaspoons rice vinegar
2 teaspoons ginger paste
2 teaspoons mirin

- Mix all ingredients together and serve in individual dipping bowls

- Toss shrimp in the lemon juice. Stage all the ingredients on the counter so you can easily assemble the rolls.

- Soak one rice paper wrapper in water until it becomes soft (about 30 seconds). Be careful not to over soak since the paper will tear easily and be difficult to work with.

- Lay the soaked wrapper on a dry, clean dish towel. Two inches from one end, create a pile of the mixed ingredients. Should be about 1 inch wide and 1 inch tall and just long enough to leave 2 inches of wrapper exposed on either side.

- Fold the sides in and carefully roll the wrapper around the ingredients. Roll all the way to the end tucking in any side pieces. Try to be firm without tearing the paper.

- Cut roll in half on an angle. Repeat for the next 3 rolls.

- Serve with any left over shrimp and dipping sauce on each plate.

eat this with...
Ancient Peaks Sauvignon Blanc
Castoro Cellars Pinot Grigio
Clavo Cellars Sauvingon Blanc
Eberle Pinot Grigio
Eos Pinot Blanc
J. Lohr Riesling
JUSTIN Sauvignon Blanc
Meridian Riesling
Opolo Pinot Grigio
Robert Hall Sauvignon Blanc
Still Waters Pinot Grigio
Tablas Creek Picpoul Blanc

eat this with...
Caliza Tempranillo
Castoro Tempranillo
Edward Sellers Tempranillo
Epoch Tempranillo
Graveyard Paso Tombstone Red
Hearst Ranch Tempranillo
Tobin James Tempranillo

chorizo stuffed peppers

You can use almost any type of peppers for this recipe. Bell peppers are the most colorful and are the perfect size for an appetizer portion.

Serves 6

Chorizo Stuffing

> **2 tablespoons olive oil**
> **1 medium onion, finely chopped**
> **1 cup chopped button mushrooms**
> **1 cup chopped baby bella mushrooms**
> **1 teaspoon dried thyme**
> **Salt to taste**
> **¾ pound chorizo (bulk or remove casing)**

Rice

> **1 cup white basmati rice**
> **2 cups water**
> **Zest of 1 lime**
> **¼ teaspoon salt**
> **¼ cup chopped fresh cilantro**
> **6 medium peppers**
> **¾ cup shredded manchego cheese**
> **Cilantro for garnish (optional)**

- Preheat oven to 350F.

- Bring 2 cups of water to boil. Add salt, lime zest and rice. Bring back to a boil then reduce heat to simmer, cover and simmer for 12 minutes or until all water is absorbed. Fluff rice with a fork and stir in cilantro. Set aside until ready to stuff peppers.

- In a medium pan, heat olive oil over medium heat. Add onions and stir until they begin to soften. Stir in mushrooms. When mushrooms begin to release their juice add thyme and salt. Add chorizo to pan and continue to stir until well combined. Reduce heat to simmer and cook for an additional 10 minutes, stirring occasionally.

- If using bell peppers, chop tops off peppers and remove all seeds and membrane. If using Poblano or other peppers of similar shape, cut pepper in half horizontally and remove all seeds and membrane.

- Stuff the peppers by first spooning rice into the bottoms of the peppers (approximately 1 tablespoon for Poblano or 3 tablespoons for bell peppers) and then add chorizo mixture – the peppers should be filled to the top.

- Place peppers on a baking sheet and bake for 15 minutes. Add cheese and bake an additional 5 minutes to melt cheese (if you like a golden topping place pan under broiler for 1 minute). The peppers should be soft yet still retain their shape.

thai satay

This is one of those recipes that works well with chicken, beef or tofu. The sauce is so good you may want to make a double batch and try it with other meats and vegetables.

Serves 4

- 1 pound chicken, beef or extra firm tofu, cut into strips

Marinade

- 4 cloves garlic, minced
- 1 tablespoon light brown sugar
- Juice of 2 limes
- 1 tablespoon fish sauce
- 1 teaspoon tamarind pulp dissolved in 2 tablespoons hot water
- 2 tablespoons olive oil

Peanut Sauce

- 1 cup crunchy peanut butter
- 1 onion, finely chopped
- 1 cup "thick" coconut milk
- 1 tablespoon light brown sugar
- 1 tablespoon fish sauce
- 1 tablespoon soy sauce
- 2 teaspoons cayenne pepper
- 1 teaspoon crushed red chile peppers
- 1 stalk lemon grass, finely chopped

- Place all marinade ingredients in a blender and puree until smooth.
- Place chicken, beef or tofu in a ziplock bag. Pour marinade over items in the bag, shake to coat and zip bag closed. Marinate in refrigerator for 1 hour.
- Soak wooden skewers in water for 30 minutes. Place marinated ingredients on skewers and grill until cooked to desired level.
- Heat peanut sauce over medium heat, stir frequently and do not allow sauce to boil.
- Serve skewers with sauce for dipping or drizzle sauce over skewers.

eat this with...

Calcareous Chardonnay
Clayhouse Chenin Blanc
J&J Cellars Sparkling
J. Lohr Riesling
Le Vigne Sparkling
Mitchella Roussanne
Pear Valley Tom's Chardonnay
Robert Hall Chardonnay

chicken vol au vent

This is an upscale version of chicken pot pie and a great way to use up any leftover chicken or turkey.

Serves 6

1 package vol au vent puff pastry
1 tablespoon butter
1 tablespoon olive oil
1/2 cup sliced button mushrooms
1/4 red bell pepper, chopped
1/2 small onion, chopped
1/4 teaspoon ground sage
1/4 cup brandy
2 cups chicken, cooked and cubed
1 cup heavy cream
Salt to taste
2 tablespoons chopped fresh parsley

- Bake the puff pastry shells following package directions.
- In a large pan heat butter and olive oil.
- Sauté mushrooms, pepper and onions with sage for 5 minutes. Add brandy and simmer for 10 minutes. Add chicken and simmer for 5 more minutes.
- Stir in heavy cream. Continue to stir until all ingredients are coated and the cream is warm.
- Serve in pastry shells garnished with parsley.

eat this with...

Anglim Viognier
Calcareous Chardonnay
Caliza Viognier
Cass Viognier
Graveyard Paso Tombstone White
Halter Ranch Viognier
Kenneth Volk Chardonnay
Pear Valley Our Daily White
Venteux Viognier
Vina Robles White 4

sautéed frog legs

Frog legs are extremely popular for appetizers in many regions. They are a little more difficult to find in California, with a few people not adventurous enough to try them. I find them tasty!

Serves 4

1 tablespoon all purpose flour
Salt and pepper to taste
1 teaspoon dried thyme
4 pairs of frog legs
2 tablespoons olive oil
2 cloves garlic, finely chopped
3/4 cup dry white wine
1 tablespoon capers

- Mix flour, salt, pepper and thyme together. Lightly coat frog legs with flour mixture.
- Heat oil in a large frying pan. Over high heat, sauté the frog legs until they are golden brown on all sides. Add the garlic and sauté for 1 more minute.
- Add the wine and capers to the pan. Stir and reduce heat to low. Allow legs to cook in simmering wine for 10 minutes, flipping legs after 5 minutes.
- Serve legs on a bed of lettuce, asian slaw or fried rice.

eat this with...

Ancient Peaks Sauvignon Blanc
Clavo Cellars Sauvignon Blanc
Halter Ranch Sauvignon Blanc
J&J Cellars Sparking
Kenneth Volk Verdelho
Le Vigne Sparkling
Pear Valley Sauvingon Blanc
Pretty-Smith Sauvignon Blanc
Robert Hall Sauvignon Blanc
Tobin James Sauvignon Blanc
Wild Horse Verdelho

petite top sirloin burgers by Mitchella Vineyard & Winery

These petite top sirloin burgers with rustic cheddar, caramelized onions and heirloom tomatoes are perfect for a garden luncheon.

approximately 40 mini burgers

2 ½ pounds fresh ground top sirloin
8 ounces assorted wild mushrooms
1/3 cup high quality red wine
12 cloves garlic
10 slices rustic aged sharp cheddar
4-6 small heirloom tomatoes
2 medium sweet onions
1 cup fresh aioli or mayonnaise

1 tablespoon salt
2 tablespoons ground cumin
4 tablespoons olive oil
2 tablespoons balsamic vinegar
2 tablespoons dark brown sugar
1 pound butter
2 baguettes (San Luis Sourdough)
1 cup arugula

> **eat this with...**
> Mitchella Shameless

- Coarsely chop six cloves of garlic and sauté in 2 tablespoons of olive oil. Coarsely chop the mushrooms and add to the garlic, continue sautéing for 10 minutes, add 1/3 cup red wine, simmer until liquid is reduced. Remove, and cool mushrooms in large mixing bowl.

- Thinly slice onions and sauté in 2 tablespoons of olive oil until a light golden brown, about 15 minutes. Carefully add 2 tablespoons of balsamic vinegar stir until reduced. Quickly add, still stirring, 2 tablespoons of brown sugar, simmer until caramelized, about 7 minutes. Remove to small bowl and cover.

- Add 1 tablespoon cumin to one cup of aioli or mayonnaise, mix well, refrigerate. Quarter the slices of cheddar cheese. Slice the tomatoes into 2-3" rounds. Slice the sourdough baguettes into ¼ inch slices.

- Add 1 tablespoon cumin to cooled mushrooms, 1 tablespoon salt, and fresh ground sirloin. Mix and form into small patties, just less than 1/8 cup per patty. Add butter and 6 cloves of garlic to heat proof pan on BBQ, add sliced sourdough, grill on BBQ until golden brown. Grill hamburgers for 2 minutes, turn, add cheese, remove when cheese has melted.

- Assembly: Sliced sourdough, 1 teaspoon cumin aioli, burger with cheese, heirloom tomato, caramelized onion, arugula, then top with sliced sourdough.

eggplant towers

This recipe takes a fair amount of work but I think the end result is worth the effort.

2 medium eggplants
2 large red bell peppers, cut into quarters
3 tablespoons olive oil
2 cloves of garlic, minced
3 cups of baby bella mushrooms, sliced
1 tablespoon dried oregano
1/2 teaspoon cayenne pepper
1 teaspoon dried thyme
3 cups of diced, canned tomatoes

1 cup of dry red wine
1 pound ground lamb
1 medium onion, peeled and coarsely chopped
2 tablespoons tomato paste
1 tablespoon dried rosemary
1 teaspoon dried thyme
1 cup grated Pecorino Romano
Salt and Pepper to taste

eat this with...

Calcareous Syrah
Clayhouse Syrah
Cypher Tempranillo
Denner Syrah
Derby Syrah
Edward Sellers Tempranillo
Epoch Tempranillo
Locatelli Malbec
Pear Valley Malbec
Silver Horse Malbec
Starr Ranch Tempranillo
Tobin James Reserve Syrah

Chapter 3 - Small Plates

- Cut eggplant into 3/4-inch slices. Salt eggplant slices and let them sit for 30 minutes to remove any bitterness

- Coat the bottom of a medium sized sauce pan with olive oil, heat oil and add garlic. Sauté until garlic begins to brown, add mushroom and continue to sauté until mushrooms begin to release their juice then add oregano, cayenne pepper, thyme and salt, stir for 1-2 minutes to coat mushrooms and allow them to absorb flavors. Add red wine and tomatoes reserving ½ cup of tomato juice for lamb mixture. Bring to a boil then reduce heat to simmer. Allow sauce to simmer and reduce naturally while you prepare the other elements of the towers – stir occasionally.

- Rinse the salt from the eggplant, pat dry then lightly coat both sides of the eggplant slices and the red pepper with olive oil and a little salt. Place eggplant and peppers on baking sheets (covered with foil for easier clean-up) and roast in oven preheated to 400F. Peppers should be skin side up. Turn eggplant slices after 10 minutes of roasting and roast for approximately 5 more minutes then remove from oven (take care not to over cook eggplant – they should still be somewhat firm).

- When pepper skins turn black remove from oven and place in a plastic bag and allow to steam so the skins can be easily removed. Once the peppers have cooled, remove skins. Reduce oven heat to 350F.

- In a large frying pan, heat approximately 1 tablespoon of olive oil and sauté the chopped onion until it becomes translucent. Add ground lamb and stir until meat just begins to brown then add rosemary, thyme, salt and pepper. Continue to stir and add the reserved tomato juice. Simmer the lamb with herbs and juice for 5-10 minutes then stir in tomato paste and allow to simmer for an additional 10 minutes.

- Lightly grease a large baking dish then place eggplant slices along the bottom of the dish – leave room between slices as you want stand alone towers. Spoon lamb mixture onto each eggplant slice approximately ½ inch thick. Place another slice of eggplant on top of the lamb mixture, spoon mushroom sauce over eggplant approximately ½ inch thick, place another eggplant slice on top, place roasted pepper on top and drizzle a little of the mushroom sauce over top – then sprinkle cheese on top of each tower. Bake in oven preheated to 350F for 30 minutes.

Salads

If you think salads are difficult to pair with wines...think again. Adding mushrooms, cheese, fruit, fish or meat can often make a huge difference in how well the salad will pair with wine.

asian slaw - 66

japhen chopped salad - 67

butter lettuce salad - 68

curried fruit and nut salad - 69

la salade lyonnais - 70

grilled shrimp caesar - 73

sautéed scallops with orange sauce - 74

arugula & shaved parmesan salad - 75

shitake bacon salad - 77

brown rice-chickpea salad - 78

bufala mozzarella and heirloom tomatoes - 79

spinach and strawberry salad - 80

crab louis - 81

crab orzo salad - 82

taco salad - 83

grilled vegetable salad - 84

roasted root vegetable salad - 85

asian slaw

This is a great salad to serve as a base for grilled shrimp, asian-style chicken or pan seared fish. I have even served it with sautéd frog legs on top. Makes a nice, crispy side to accompany most Asian meals.

Serves 4
- 2 cups shredded Napa cabbage
- 1 cup julienne cut carrots
- 1 cup julienne cut broccoli stalks
- 2 tablespoons toasted sesame seeds (optional)

Dressing
- 2 tablespoons sesame oil
- 1 tablespoon rice vinegar
- 1 tablespoon mirin
- 1 tablespoon soy sauce
- 1 teaspoon Sriracha hot chili sauce (optional)

- In a small bowl whisk together all dressing ingredients

- Pour dressing over vegetables and toss to lightly coat

eat this with...
Anglim Roussanne
Eos Pinot Blanc
Hearthstone Pearl
Le Vigne Chardonnay
Orchid Hill Grenache Rosé
Pretty-Smith Sauvignon Blanc
Tobin James Chardonnay

japhen chopped salad by Steve Kroener, Silver Horse

Steve makes this salad for large parties and it is always a big hit. Given that he named the salad as a combination of "Jane" (the love of his life) and "Stephen", you know this is one of his favorites.

Salad - serves 32

      1 large bag of shredded carrots

      6 heads of romaine cut sideways into ribbons

      2 pounds fresh mozzarella, shredded

      3 small cans of Garbanzo beans, drained

      2 packages pearl tomatoes, sliced into halves

      4 bunches scallions, sliced

      1 large eggplant, cut into 1/2 inch slices with skin left on and grilled in olive oil

      2 medium jicama, peeled and cubed into one inch slices

      2 pounds shrimp, grilled (optional)

Dressing

      1/3 cup red wine vinegar

      3/4 cup olive oil

      Dijon mustard, to taste

      Balsamic vinegar, to taste

      Salt and pepper, to taste

- Mix all salad ingredients together in a large bowl and place in fridge.
- Whisk together all dressing ingredients. Pour dressing on top of salad or serve on the side if you prefer.

eat this with...
Silver Horse Albariño

butter lettuce salad by Niels & Bimmer Udsen, Castoro Cellars

This easy to prepare salad has a wonderful mix of textures, colors and flavors.

Serves 4

> 1 head butter lettuce
> 1 apple, sliced
> ½ cup walnuts
> ¼ pound gorgonzola, crumbled
> 1-2 tablespoons walnut oil
> Balsamic vinegar , to taste
> ¼ to ½ cup pomegranate seeds

- ❧ Break up the lettuce in a large salad bowl. Add cheese, nuts, oil and vinegar then toss.
- ❧ Garnish with the pomegranate seeds (optional).

eat this with...
Castoro Cellars Viognier
Castoro Cellars Fumé Blanc

Chapter 4 - Salads

curried fruit and nut salad

The onion and curry flavors in the dressing play with the fruit and nuts in this salad. With fresh spinach from the farmers' market this salad is beautiful and healthy. One of my summer favorites.

Serves 6

3 cups torn romaine lettuce leaves
3 cups torn fresh spinach leaves
1 cup green seedless grapes, halved
1 15 ounce can mandarin orange segments, drained
1/2 cup toasted sliced almonds

❧ In a large bowl combine all the above ingredients and refrigerate until ready to dress and serve.

Dressing (makes one cup)

1/2 cup olive oil
1/4 cup white wine vinegar
1/4 cup chopped green onions
2 tablespoons packed light brown sugar
2 teaspoons curry powder
1 teaspoon soy sauce

❧ Blend the above ingredients, adding more curry if desired. Just before serving whisk dressing to blend and pour enough over the salad to lightly coat.

eat this with...

Bodegas Paso Robles Galicia
Caliza Viognier
Pear Valley Our Daily White
Penman Springs Dry Humor
Oso Libre Viognier
Pipestone Viognier
San Marcos Creek White Merlot
Silver Horse Albariño
Wildhorse Verdelho

la salade lyonnais by Chef Jacob, Cass Winery

House-cured bacon, soft poached egg on a frisée bed with Dijon vinaigrette.

Bacon

5 pounds fresh pork belly (Berkshire if you can find it)
1/4 cup coarse kosher salt
2 teaspoons pink curing salt #1
   (your butcher will know exactly what this is)
4 tablespoons coarsely ground black pepper
4 bay leaves, crumbled
1 teaspoon freshly grated nutmeg
1/4 cup brown sugar or honey or maple syrup
5 cloves of garlic, smashed with the flat side of a chef's knife
2 tablespoons juniper berries, lightly crushed (optional)
5 to 10 sprigs fresh thyme (optional)

- Put your belly in a zip-top bag or on a sheet tray or in a plastic container. Rub the salt and spice mixture all over the belly. Close the bag or cover it with plastic wrap, and stick it in the refrigerator for seven days (get your hands in there and give the spices another good rubbing around midway through).

- After seven days, take it out of the fridge, rinse off all the seasonings under cold water and pat it dry. Put it on a sheet tray and put it in the oven (put it on a rack on a sheet tray if you have one) and turn the oven on to 200F. Leave it in the oven for 90 minutes (or, if you want to measure the internal temperature, until it reaches 150 degrees F.). Let it cool and refrigerate it until you're ready to cook it. Congratulations! It's bacon!

A word about curing bacon from Chef Jacob: *"There are 2 basic methods of curing pork belly (bacon). A wet method (brining) and a dry method. I used the dry method for this dish. It involves rubbing the pork belly with a salt/curing salt mix (and aromatics) and allowing it to sit in refrigeration for a week, covered. Pork belly is STILL not widely available in grocery stores (A tragedy to this pork-crazed chef!), so, if you do not have a farmed source for pork products, I would go to your local butcher and ask them. If they don't carry it, they will surely know where to get it. Do this several days in advance, as it may take some time."*

Chapter 4 - Salads

Dijon vinaigrette

>   **4 tablespoons sherry vinegar**
>   **1 tablespoon minced shallot**
>   **1 tablespoon Dijon mustard**
>   **2/3 cup extra-virgin olive oil**
>   **Salt and freshly ground pepper, to taste**

Salad

>   **6 slices of your homemade bacon,**
>   **cooked, cut in half**
>   **4 poached eggs**
>   **4 bunches of frisee**
>   **4 slices of french bread cut in half, seasoned**
>   **with salt, pepper & olive oil and toasted**
>   **into large croutons**

- In a small bowl, whisk the sherry vinegar with the shallot and Dijon mustard. In a thin, steady stream, whisk in the olive oil until emulsified. Season with salt and pepper.

- Assemble the salad by laying the frisee down in the center of the plate. Top with the poached egg in the center. Lean the ½ bacon slices and croutons around the salad. Alternating between the two. Three slices of each per salad will do. Drizzle vinaigrette over entire salad.

eat this with...
Cass Rockin One - a blend of
Mourvèdre, Grenache, and Syrah

grilled shrimp caesar by Mitchella Vineyard & Winery

This caesar salad by Mitchella Vineyard & Winery is loaded with flavor.
After you make this recipe you will never go back to packaged caesar dressing again.

Shrimp
- 1 pound shrimp (21/25 count)
- ½ cup Mitchella Viognier
- 3 cloves garlic, minced
- ½ tablespoon ground black pepper
- ½ tablespoon ground cumin
- ½ tablespoon ground oregano
- 1 tablespoon lemon zest
- 2 tablespoons of fresh lemon juice
- 1 tablespoon brown sugar
- 2 tablespoons olive oil

Dressing
- ¼ cup egg beaters
- 1 clove garlic, minced
- 1 teaspoon anchovy paste (optional)
- 2 teaspoons Dijon mustard
- 2 tablespoons tarragon vinegar
- ½ teaspoon Worcestershire sauce
- 3 tablespoons olive oil
- ¼ cup finely grated parmesan
- Salt and pepper to taste

Salad
- 3 hearts of romaine, cleaned and chopped
- 2 cups croutons (4-5 ounces)
- ½ cup shaved parmesan cheese

- Clean the shrimp and butterfly. Marinate in the wine, garlic, black pepper, cumin, ground oregano, lemon zest, lemon juice, brown sugar and olive oil for 30 minutes to 1 hour. Grill for 2-3 minutes on each side, do not over-cook.

- In a bowl, whisk together the egg beaters, garlic, anchovy paste, mustard, vinegar, and Worcestershire sauce. Slowly add the olive oil in a steady stream, whisking the whole time. Stir in the Parmesan and season with salt and pepper.

- In a large bowl, toss the dressing with the lettuce until well coated. Add the croutons and toss to combine. Arrange the grilled shrimp on top and sprinkle with the shaved parmesan. Top with salt and fresh black pepper to taste.

eat this with...
Mitchella Viognier

sautéed scallops with orange sauce

Scallops are yet another wonderful item to include in a salad that is to be served with wine. Use the warm sauce from the scallops to dress the crisp greens.

Serves 4

- 12 large sea scallops
- 2 tablespoons olive oil
- 2 cloves garlic, minced
- 2 green onions, chopped
- 1/2 red bell pepper, chopped
- 1 tablespoon soy sauce
- Juice of one orange
- 1/2 teaspoon orange zest
- 2 teaspoons fresh thyme
- 1/2 teaspoon cayenne pepper
- 4 orange slices
- Salt and ground pepper to taste
- 6 cups mixed lettuce

- Heat olive oil in large frying pan
- Pat scallops to remove any moisture, sprinkle with salt and saute just long enough to brown on both sides -- they should not be cooked through. Remove from pan while preparing the other warm ingredients.
- Saute garlic, onions and peppers until peppers begin to soften then stir in soy sauce, orange juice, zest, thyme and pepper. Simmer until sauce reduces by 1/3.
- Add scallops back in to warm them and continuing cooking through (approximately 3 minutes).
- Plating: Place lettuce in individual bowls, place scallops and peppers on top then drizzle the sauce over each bowl. Garnish with orange slices and season with ground black pepper and salt.

eat this with...

Adelaida Viognier
Anglim Marsanne
Calcareous Viognier/Marsanne
Cass Rockin One Blanc
Graveyard Paso Tombstone White
J Dusi Pinot Gris
Pomar Junction Viognier
Tablas Creek Marsanne

Chapter 4 - Salads

arugula & shaved parmesan salad

Spicy arugula with salty parmesan in a simple Tuscan vinaigrette is a nice wine friendly salad. Add candied walnuts or roasted mushrooms to fit with your taste preferences and the rest of your meal.

Salad (serves 4-6)
>   6 cups fresh arugula
>   1 cup shaved Parmigiano Reggiano
>   2 tablespoons toasted pine nuts (optional)

Tuscan vinaigrette
>   3/4 cup extra-virgin olive oil
>   2 tablespoons red wine vinegar
>   1 garlic clove, minced
>   2 teaspoons dried thyme
>   Salt and freshly ground black pepper to taste

- In a small bowl whisk together the vinaigrette ingredients until well blended.

- In a large salad bowl toss together arugula and cheese.

- Add vinaigrette to salad gradually, tossing after each addition. The salad is best when very lightly dressed so the spice flavor of the arugula shines through.

- Garnish with pine nuts if desired.

eat this with...

AronHill Melange de Blanc
Caliza Primitivo
Chateaux Margene Sangiovese
Derby Pinot Gris
Eos Pinot Blanc
Tobin James Sangiovese
Wild Horse Pinot Noir
Windward Pinot Noir

shitake bacon salad by Maggie D'Ambrosia, Windward Vineyard

Chef Charles D. Paladin Wayne served this at Windward Vineyard for a Central Coast Wine Classic Dinner. It was a huge success and loved by each guest. Windward Vineyard was granted permission to share this recipe for everyone's enjoyment and Maggie has made a few changes. Combine the following four parts to create the perfect salad paired with Windward Vineyard Estate Pinot Noir.

Shitake Bacon
12 medium shitake mushroom caps, sliced paper thin
2 cups grape seed oil
Fine sea Salt

- Heat oil to 300 degrees. Line a baking sheet with paper towels. In small batches place the thinly sliced shitake into the oil and fry to a crisp stage then remove to the paper towels to absorb excess oil and lightly sprinkle with sea salt.

***Store in a sealed container in a cool place for up to two months. Lightly heat in a 350 degree oven before using to restore crispness.*

Candied Garlic
1 cup sugar
1 cup Chardonnay (Maggie uses Pinot Noir)
1 cup peeled fresh garlic cloves, ends trimmed

- In a sauce pan dissolve the sugar in the wine and add the garlic cloves.
- Bring to a slow rolling boil and watch for the cloves to become translucent and lightly tan colored. Set aside to cool.

*** *Can be stored in refrigerator for up to 6 months*

Garlic Syrup and Sherry Vinaigrette
½ cup candied garlic (reserve syrup)
1/8 cup reserved candied garlic syrup
1/8 cup Banyuls sherry vinegar (or your favorite)
1/4 cup extra virgin olive oil
½ teaspoon salt
½ teaspoon pepper

- Place all ingredients into a shaker and shake to combine.

Salad
12 ounces Mache salad (Trader Joes)
1 cup baby heirloom tomatoes cut in half
½ cup sheep feta cheese crumbled
¼ cup dressing
½ ounce Shitake Bacon

- Toss Mache in salad bowl with dressing. Add tomatoes, garlic, feta, and Shitake Bacon.

eat this with...
Windward Vineyard Estate Pinot Noir

brown rice-chickpea salad

by Michele Knecht, Seasonal Custom Cuisine

This Brown Rice-Chickpea Salad with Herb de Provence recipe by Michele is a client favorite and on her menu every week. Make this at home and feel good about serving a tasty and oh so very healthy meal.

eat this with...

Anglim Viognier
Eberle Rosé
Halter Ranch Grenache
HammerSky Rosé
Kenneth Volk Malvasia Bianca
L'Aventure Rosé
Pretty-Smith Palette de Rouge

Salad (makes 6 cups)

1 cup short grain brown rice
2 cups water
1 cup chick peas, cooked
¼ cup diced celery
¼ cup diced carrot
¼ cup fresh cooked or frozen corn, thawed
¼ cup frozen peas, thawed
1-2 tablespoons finely chopped parsley

- Bring rice & water to boil, cover and lower heat. Simmer for 45 minutes. Remove from heat. Place a clean towel under lid, across top of pan & replace lid(to absorb moisture) let sit an additional 10-15 minutes to steam. Fluff rice and let cool to room temperature.
- Combine remaining ingredients with rice.

Dressing

2 tablespoons finely minced shallot
1 tablespoon Herbes de Provence
1 teaspoon Dijon mustard
1 clove garlic, finely minced
2 tablespoons red wine vinegar
1 tablespoon ume plum vinegar
2/3 cups good quality olive oil

- Combine all dressing ingredients with whisk in food processor.
- Toss with salad to taste just before serving. Extra dressing can be stored in fridge for 1 week.

~78~

Chapter 4 - Salads

bufala mozzarella and heirloom tomatoes

by Niels & Bimmer Udsen, Castoro Cellars

When you can source fresh, heirloom tomatoes, this is the recipe to make. The bright colors, natural acidity, creamy mozzarella and hint of fresh basil make a perfect start to almost any meal.

Serves 6

> 8 ounces fresh bufala mozzarella in its milk
> 1-1½ pounds vine ripe heirloom tomatoes
> 1-3 tablespoons extra virgin olive oil
> Balsamic vinegar, drizzle
> A few leaves fresh basil

- Slice tomatoes and cheese thinly.
- Alternate the ingredients on a tray and drizzle with oil and Balsamic vinegar. Let sit for a bit and enjoy.

****Can be served on toasted baguette slices*

eat this with...
Castoro Cellars Pinot Grigio
Castoro Cellars Viognier

spinach and strawberry salad

Early summer, when strawberries are nice and sweet, is the ideal time to make this salad.

Serves 6

1 pint fresh strawberries, sliced
1/4 cup balsamic vinegar
1/3 cup olive oil
7 cups spinach leaves, torn
1/4 cup fresh mint leaves, chopped
1/2 cup feta or blue cheese crumbles
Salt & pepper to taste

- Pour vinegar over strawberries in a glass bowl. Cover and let marinate for 1 hour.

- Remove strawberries from juice, reserving for later use. Whisk oil with juice until well integrated.

- Toss together spinach, mint and feta. Add enough dressing to lightly coat, add salt and pepper to taste then toss again.

eat this with...

Adelaida Viognier
Ancient Peaks Sauvignon Blanc
Calcareous Rosé
Caliza Rosé
Chronic Cellars Riesling
DAOU Viognier
Halter Ranch Rosé
Opolo Viognier
Pear Valley Rosé
Pomar Junction Viognier
Robert Hall Viognier
Wild Horse Viognier

crab louis

The secret to a good crab louis is the dressing. Don't even think about buying store bought thousand island dressing -- a true louis dressing should have a little kick and doesn't take long to prepare. The presentation can also be spectacular with all the colors on the plate -- for fun let your guests compose their own plate.

Serves 4

- 4 hard boiled eggs, sliced
- 1/2 cup black olives, sliced
- 4 large crab legs, cut into 1-2 inch pieces
- 4 green onions, chopped
- 1 avocado sliced
- 2 tomatoes, cut into wedges
- 1 medium cucumber, peeled & sliced
- 1 head iceberg lettuce
- 1 lemon, cut into wedges

Dressing

- 1 cup mayonnaise
- 1 small tomato, finely diced
- Juice from 1/2 lemon
- 1 teaspoon Sriracha Hot Chili Sauce
- 1 teaspoon prepared horseradish
- 1 medium scallion, minced
- 2 tablespoons green olives, finely chopped
- Salt to taste

- ❧ Whisk together all dressing ingredients. This can be done a day ahead with dressing stored in a sealed container and refrigerated after whisking.
- ❧ Compose salad ingredients on each plate and serve with dressing on the side.

eat this with...

Cass Rockin One Blanc
J. Lohr Sauvignon Blanc
Pomar Junction Viognier
Robert Hall Sauvignon Blanc
Tablas Creek Côtes de Tablas Blanc
Wild Horse Verdelho

crab orzo salad

My crab salad recipe is a little challenging to pair with wine since it has a high level of acidity due to the lemon dressing as well as a lot of heat from the Dijon mustard and hot sauce. On top of that the wine has to complement the rich crab meat. I find the Rhône blends to work best.. avoid white wines with really high acidity for this recipe!

Serves 4
 Dressing
   Juice of 1 lemon
   2 tablespoons Dijon mustard
   1 tablespoon Sriracha hot chili sauce
 Salad
   2 cups of orzo cooked and chilled
   ½ red pepper finely diced
   ¼ cup chopped spinach
   2 large basil leaves finely chopped
   4 large crab legs (canned crab may be substituted)
   1 small head butter lettuce
   1 lemon

- In a small bowl whisk together dressing ingredients.

- Toss all salad ingredients in a large bowl. Pour dressing over top and toss again. Refrigerate the salad for at least 1 hour to allow the flavors to combine.

- When ready to serve place salad on a bed of butter lettuce with a lemon wedge on top.

eat this with...

Bodegas Paso Robles Doña Blanca
Eberle Côtes-du-Rôbles Blanc
Graveyard Paso Tombstone Pink
Le Vigne Sparkling
Tablas Creek Esprit De Beaucastel Blanc
Robert Hall Grenache Blanc
Wild Horse Malvasia Bianca

Chapter 4 - Salads

taco salad

This is a great way to use up leftover chili. Sometimes I make a pot of chili just to have taco salads.

Serves 2 as an entrée
4 cups of mixed greens (spinach is great with this)
2 cups homemade chili (see recipe page 100)
1 cup shredded Mexican mix or sharp cheddar cheese
24 tortilla chips

- Heat chili on stove top or microwave.
- Divide greens on plates and top with hot chili.
- Sprinkle cheese on top and place chips around the side of the salad.

eat this with...
Castoro Cellars Gewurztraminer
DAOU Zinfandel
J&J Cellars Malbec
Le Vigne Sparkling
Locatelli Malbec
Pear Valley Malbec
Ranchita Canyon Malbec
San Marcos Creek Zinfandel
Silver Horse Malbec
Steinbeck Vineyards Zinfandel
Wild Horse Zinfandel

grilled vegetable salad

The combination of the grilled vegetables with fresh greens is very nice for a summer salad. The grilled vegetables can be warm, room temperature or even cold if you had leftovers from a last night's dinner.

Serves 2

4 cups of mixed greens
2 tablespoons olive oil
2 cups grilled vegetables (see recipe page 149)
1/2 cup grated parmesan cheese
Fresh ground black pepper, to taste

- In a large bowl toss the greens in olive oil. Add the grilled vegetables and toss again.

- Plate each salad and top with cheese and fresh ground black pepper.

eat this with...

Ancient Peaks Sauvignon Blanc
Castoro Cellars Pinot Blanc
Clayhouse Chenin Blanc
Derby Pinot Gris
Eberle Pinot Grigio
Halter Ranch Sauvignon Blanc
Pear Valley Sauvignon Blanc
Robert Hall Sauvignon Blanc
Still Waters Sauvignon Blanc
Tobin James Sauvingon Blanc

Chapter 4 - Salads

roasted root vegetable salad

In the fall and winter I tend to roast large pots of vegetables. Roasted root vegetables and garlic are terrific with fresh greens. The vegetables can be warm, room temperature or cold.

Serves 2

4 cups of mixed greens
2 tablespoons olive oil
2 cups roasted vegetables (see recipe page148)
1/2 cup fresh goat cheese, crumbled
Fresh ground black pepper, to taste

- In a large bowl toss the greens in olive oil. Add the roasted vegetables and cheese, then toss again.
- Serve in salad bowl topped with fresh ground pepper.

eat this with...

Castoro Cellars Gewurztraminer
Chronic Cellars Riesling
Eos Merlot
J. Lohr Riesling
Le Vigne Merlot
Meridian Gewurztraminer
Pear Valley Merlot
Riverstar Merlot
Tobin James Merlot

Soups, Stews & Chili

A bowl of something flavorful and warm is what I call comfort food. Whenever the weather turns a little wet or cold (keep in mind I live in Paso Robles, so if any of my Canadian relatives are reading this please don't laugh), I tend to make a large pot of soup, stew or chili. You will also find a couple of cold soup recipes for the warmer days included in the beginning of this chapter.

roasted garlic and almond soup

by Chef Marc LeDuc, Tobin James Cellars

This cold soup is perfect with a sandwich or salad for a light summer lunch or as a refreshing soup course before firing up the grill in the evening.

Serves 4

8 ounces roasted skinless almonds
1 quart vegetable stock or broth
4 ounces spice vinegar (Chaparral Gardens)
20 cloves of roasted garlic
Salt and pepper, to taste
20 green grapes, sliced thin
2 tablespoons extra virgin olive oil

eat this with...
Tobin James Reserve Chardonnay
Tobin James Paradise Syrah Rosé

- Put all ingredients except for the grapes and the olive oil into a high power blender(I use a Vita Prep) and blend on the highest speed for 2 minutes or until smooth.
- If soup is too thick add some vegetable stock. Season with salt and pepper and chill for two hours.
- Serve in a chilled bowl and garnish with the sliced green grapes and olive oil.

Chapter 5 - Soups, stews & chili

la soupe froide de pois by Chef Jacob, Cass Catering

Cold pea soup, crispy shallots and blue crab claws. This recipe from Chef Jacob blends some wonderful flavors sure to delight your dining companions.

2 tablespoons unsalted butter
2 cups chopped leeks, white and light green parts (2 leeks)
1 cup chopped yellow onion
4 cups chicken stock, preferably homemade
5 cups freshly shelled English peas
2/3 cup chopped fresh mint leaves, loosely packed

2 teaspoons kosher salt
1/2 teaspoon freshly ground black pepper
1/2 cup freshly chopped chives
½ cup creme fraiche
¼ pound fresh blue crab claw meat
3 shallots, peeled and sliced thinly in a mandolin
¼ cup flour
¼ teaspoon each of salt and pepper
Vegetable oil for frying

∾ For the shallots. Combine the flour, salt and pepper in a medium size bowl. Make sure it's big enough to toss the shallots around in. Heat the oil in a high-sided pan to 350F. Once it reaches that temperature, toss the shallots in the flour mixture. Sift of any residual flour and carefully add them to the hot oil. Fry in batches until light brown and bubbles have subsided. Make sure to allow the oil to return to 350F before you fry your next batch. Remove with a slotted spoon or a small strainer and let them drain on a paper towel. Sprinkle a pinch of salt on them as they cool.

eat this with...
Cass Roussanne

∾ For the soup: Heat the butter in a large saucepan, add the leeks and onion, and cook over medium-low heat for 5 to 10 minutes, until the onion is tender. Add the chicken stock, increase the heat to high, and bring to a boil. Add the peas and cook for 3 to 5 minutes, until the peas are tender. Off the heat, add the mint, salt, and pepper. Puree the soup in batches: place 1 cup of soup in a blender, place the lid on top, and puree on low speed. With the blender still running, open the vent hole in the lid and slowly add more soup until the blender is three-quarters full. Pour the soup into a large bowl and repeat until all the soup is pureed. Put it in the fridge until fully chilled. Whisk in the creme fraiche and chives and taste for seasoning. Ladle the soup into bowls and top with a small pile of crab. Add the crispy shallots on top as garnish and serve

roasted tomato and pepper soup

The roasted vegetables load this soup with flavor. So simple to make, yet your guests will think you worked for hours to get all the flavor in the bowl.

Serves 6

- **6 red bell peppers, halved and seeded**
- **1 large onion, peeled and chopped**
- **6 large tomatoes**
- **8 cloves of garlic, peeled**
- **1/4 cup olive oil**
- **Salt & pepper, to taste**
- **6 cups chicken stock**
- **1/4 cup chopped fresh basil**

- Preheat oven to 400F

- Place peppers, onion, tomatoes, garlic and oil in a dutch oven. Stir to coat vegetables with olive oil and season with salt and pepper. Roast in oven for 45 minutes.

- Remove from oven and place on stove top. Add chicken stock and bring to a boil. Reduce heat and simmer for 15 minutes.

- Using a hand blender, puree the solids until smooth. Adjust seasoning if required.

- Serve garnished with fresh basil.

eat this with...

Calcareous Syrah
Cass Syrah
Eberle Sangiovese
Le Vigne Sangiovese
Niner Sangiovese
Peachy Canyon Sangiovese
Opolo Nebbiolo
San Marcos Creek Nebbiolo
Venteux Syrah
Vina Robles Syrah

Chapter 5 - Soups, stews & chili

cream of mushroom soup

The dried wild mushrooms give this soup a much richer flavor than a traditional cream of mushroom soup. Serve this as part of an elegant meal or as a lunch dish.

Serve 6

- **1 ounce dried wild mushrooms**
- **2 cups boiling water**
- **1/4 cup unsalted butter**
- **1 medium onion, chopped**
- **1/2 pound button mushrooms, sliced**
- **3 tablespoons all-purpose flour**
- **1/2 teaspoon salt**
- **1/4 cup dry sherry**
- **4 cups vegetable stock**
- **2 tablespoons soy sauce**
- **1 cup half-and-half**
- **2 tablespoons finely chopped fresh parsley**

- Boil the dried mushroom in water for 15 minutes. Leave mushrooms in the hot water to create a flavorful broth while you work on other components.

- In a medium pot, melt the butter and add the onion. Sauté the onion until soft (approximately 3 minutes). Add the button mushrooms and sauté until mushrooms begin to release their juice. Sprinkle with flour and salt. Stir for 1 minute to cook the flour and coat the mushrooms.

- Stir as you add the sherry, vegetable stock and soy sauce. Bring to a boil for 1 minute then reduce heat to simmer.

- Remove the wild mushrooms from mushroom broth. Rinse mushrooms, remove any hard stems and chop. Add mushrooms to the soup pot. Strain mushroom broth and also add to the pot. Cover and simmer for 20 minutes.

- Using a hand blender, puree the ingredients in the pot.

- Add half-and-half and simmer for 5 minutes.

- Serve garnished with parsley.

eat this with...

Calcareous Chardonnay
Castoro Cellars Pinot Noir
Clayhouse Rosé
Derby Pinot Noir
Halter Ranch Rosé
Kenneth Volk Pinot Noir
Pomar Junction Pinot Noir
Ranchita Canyon Petit Verdot
Tassajara Pinot Noir
Windward Vineyard Pinot Noir

butternut squash soup

This is a nice soup to have before a roasted chicken or turkey dinner.

Serves 4

1 tablespoon olive oil
1 large onion, chopped
2 cloves garlic, minced
1 stalk of celery, chopped
1 cup unsweetened apple juice
1 potato, peeled and diced
1 butternut squash, peeled, seeded and cubed
3 cups chicken stock
3 bay leaves
2 teaspoons dried thyme
1 teaspoon ginger paste
Salt & pepper to taste
2/3 cup heavy cream
Garnish (optional)
Sliced mushrooms sauteed in 2 tablespoons sherry with a pinch of ground marjoram

~ Heat oil in a large soup pot. Add onion, garlic and celery. Saute for 3 minutes.

~ Add apple juice. Cover and simmer for 10 minutes.

~ Add potato, squash, stock, bay leaves, thyme, ginger, salt and pepper. Bring to a boil then reduce heat, cover and simmer for 30 minutes.

~ Remove and discard bay leaves.

~ Add the evaporated milk and puree with a hand blender until smooth.

~ Serve garnished with sauteed mushrooms.

eat this with...

Calcareous Chardonnay
J. Lohr Chardonnay
Pear Valley Tom's Oak Chardonnay
Penman Springs Merlot
Tobin James Chardonnay
Wild Horse Merlot

chicken gumbo

Be sure to adjust the spice level to suit your tastes for this recipe. I like mine spicy!

Served 6

2 tablespoons olive oil
1 large onion, chopped
3 gloves of garlic, chopped
1 pound boneless, skinless chicken
    breasts, cubed
2 stalks celery, chopped
1 large carrot, peeled and chopped
1 can (28 ounces) diced tomatoes

4 cups chicken stock
1 package (10 ounces) frozen sliced okra
1 tablespoon Tabasco sauce
1 teaspoon cayenne pepper
2 teaspoons dried thyme
1 teaspoon celery seeds
Salt to taste
1/2 cup uncooked orzo
1/4 cup chopped fresh parsley (optional)

- Heat olive oil in a large pot. Saute onion and garlic for three minutes. Add chicken and saute until chicken begins to brown (approximately 5 minutes). Add celery and carrots and saute for 3 more minutes.

- Add tomatoes and chicken stock to the pot and bring to a boil. Add okra, Tabasco, pepper, thyme, celery seeds and salt. Stir and bring back to a boil. Reduce heat, cover and simmer for 45 minutes.

- Add orzo to the pot, stir and simmer for an additional 20 minutes. The orzo should be tender.

- Serve in a bowl garnished with parsley.

eat this with...

Anglim Grenache
Caliza Rosé
Castoro Cellars Gewurztraminer
Clavo Rosé
Eos Gewurztraminer
Hearthstone Grenache
Kenneth Volk Grenache
Meridian Gewurztraminer
San Marcos Creek White Merlot
Tobin James Rosé
Villicana Rosé

salmon bisque

This recipe is for salmon lovers. Be sure to use fresh, wild salmon and don't skip the dill.

Serves 6

2 tablespoons olive oil
1 tablespoon butter
1 cup thinly sliced leeks (whites only)
1 cup thinly sliced brown
    mushrooms
3 cloves garlic, minced
16 ounces clam juice
28 ounces canned tomatoes
1/4 cup chopped fresh parsley
2 teaspoons chopped fresh dill
Salt & pepper, to taste
2 cups fresh salmon, 1/2 inch cubes
2 cups milk (1% ok)
Fresh dill for garnish

∾ In a large pot heat olive oil and butter. Add leeks, mushrooms and garlic and sauté for 5 minutes.

∾ Add clam juice, tomatoes, parsley, dill and salt and pepper. Simmer for 10 minutes then add salmon and milk. Simmer for an additional 10 minutes.

∾ Remove two cups of the mixture. Using a hand blender puree the contents in the pot to thicken. Add the two cups back into the pot and stir. Adjust seasoning if required.

∾ Served garnished with fresh dill.

eat this with...

Ancient Peaks Merlot
Hearst Ranch Merlot
Kenneth Volk Merlot
Pear Valley Tom's Oak Chardonnay
Rabbit Ridge Merlot
Robert Hall merlot
San Marcos Creek Nebbiolo
Wild Horse Unbridled Chardonnay

potato leek soup

This soup is meant to be very thick. It is the kind of soup that fills and warms you on a cold, wet day.

Serves 6

3 tablespoons butter
3 leeks
4 large potatoes, peeled and sliced
3/4 cup water
2 teaspoons dried thyme
1 teaspoon ground white pepper
Salt to taste
4 cups milk
6 tablespoons chopped pancetta
1 tablespoon chopped chives

- Melt the butter in a large pot.

- Wash the leeks and remove any dried/hard green leaves. Cut in half and thinly slice, then sauté in melted butter.

- Add potatoes, water, thyme, pepper and salt to the pot. Stir, cover and cook until the potatoes and the leeks are soft (approximately 20 minutes).

- Stir in the milk and allow to warm without coming to a boil. Using a hand blender, puree until smooth.

- Serve garnished with pancetta and chives.

eat this with...

Ancient Peaks Merlot
Calcareous Chardonnay
Halter Ranch Merlot
J&J Cellars Merlot
J. Lohr Chardonnay
Peachy Canyon Merlot
Pear Valley Tom's Oak Chardonnay
Robert Hall Chardonnay
San Marcos Creek Merlot
Tobin James Merlot
Wild Horse Merlot

white bean & sausage soup

Whenever I make this soup it takes me back to some very fun times in Italy. The spicy sausage and the rich beans are an excellent pairing with several Paso Robles wines.

Serves 6

1 pound dried white beans
3 bay leaves
¼ teaspoon dried sage
2 tablespoons olive oil
5 links spicy Italian sausage
1 yellow onion, coarsely chopped
3 cloves of garlic, finely chopped

4 carrots, coarsely chopped
3 stalks of celery, coarsely chopped
5 cups chicken stock
½ teaspoon each dried sage, dried thyme, white pepper
Salt & pepper to taste
1 cup aged parmesan cheese, grated

- Rinse beans and place in pot. Fill pot 1 inch above beans with water, cover and soak for 6 hours to overnight. Drain beans, add 6 cups of fresh water, bay leaves, dried sage and a little salt. Bring to a boil and then reduce to simmer. Place lid on pot to almost cover and simmer for 1.5 hours. In a large pot heat olive oil and brown sausages on all sides. This should take approximately 10 minutes. Remove sausages and let them cool a little then cut into ¼ inch slices.

- Using the same pot and oil used to cook the sausages, sauté onions, garlic, carrots and celery for 5 minutes. Stir in chicken stock and bring to a boil. Add dried sage, thyme, white pepper and sausages.

- Remove bay leaves from bean pot and add half of the beans with liquid to the soup pot. Puree the remaining beans and liquid in the pan with a blend stick or use a blender. Add pureed bean mixture to soup pot and stir (this will give the soup an nice hearty consistency). Reduce heat and simmer for 30 minutes. Add salt and pepper then serve garnished with grated parmesan cheese.

eat this with...

Adelaida Cellars Syrah
AronHill Primitivo
Castoro Cellars Tempranillo
Denner Syrah
Linne Calodo Cellars Syrah
Mission View Padre's Choice
Niner Syrah
Oso Libre Syrah
Pear Valley Syrah
Tobin James Primitivo
Venteux Syrah
Vina Robles Syrah

nan's rabbit stew

As a little girl I have memories of my Grandmother making this hearty stew with the thick biscuit crust. Although I doubt my Grandmother used wine and all the herbs I have included, this is very close to the English style stew she made years ago in Corner Brook, Newfoundland. I hope others find this as much a satisfying, comforting meal as I do.

Serves 6

    2 rabbits cut into pieces
    Olive oil
    ¾ cup all purpose flour
    1 tablespoon dried thyme
    Dash of salt & pepper
    1 large onion, chopped
    1 bottle of red wine
    6 cups of vegetable stock
    2 tablespoons dried tarragon
    1 tablespoon each dried summer
       savory, dried sage, dried rosemary
    1 cup dried mushrooms (mixed
       types)
    2 small turnips
    4 carrots
    2 stalks of celery
    1 cup frozen peas

Crust

    2 ½ cups all purpose flour
    1 tablespoon baking powder
    ½ teaspoon salt
    ½ cup cold unsalted butter, cut into small pieces
    ¾ cup milk
    1 large egg, lightly beaten

Topping

    1 large egg, lightly beaten with 1 tablespoon milk

- Mix flour, thyme, salt and pepper together in a medium sized bowl. Cover the bottom of a heavy bottom, large pot with olive oil and heat. Wash rabbit pieces and dip in flour mixture to coat. Brown rabbit pieces in olive oil over medium heat in batches, adding oil as required. Once all rabbit pieces have been browned add onion to the pot and sauté until translucent.
- Pour the wine and vegetable stock into the pot with the onions. Bring to a boil then add the rabbit pieces and the herbs. Lower heat to a simmer. Simmer rabbit pieces in the wine stock mixture for approximately 4 hours.
- While the rabbit is stewing, rinse dried mushrooms and then soak in hot water for 15-30 minutes until well hydrated. Reserve the mushroom water for later. Chop mushrooms and other vegetables.
- At this point, the meat should be falling off the bone. De-bone the rabbit, returning meat pieces to the stock. Add reserved mushroom water and bring to a boil. Add all the vegetables except the peas and simmer for an additional 45 minutes. Taste and adjust herbs, salt and pepper to taste.
- While the vegetables are simmering preheat the oven to 400F and create the biscuit dough. Whisk together the flour, baking powder and salt. Cut the butter in to the dry ingredients until the mixture resembles coarse crumbs. Add milk and slightly beaten egg and stir until combined – it should be sticky and lumpy.
- Place mixture on a lightly floured surface, dust your hands with flour and knead the dough gently until it comes together. Roll out dough into one large piece that will fit over the stew.
- Remove pot from stove, stir in frozen peas and cover stew with biscuit dough. Brush with egg and milk then bake in the pre-heated oven for 20 -30 minutes. The top should be golden brown and a toothpick inserted into the crust should come out clean.
- Serve in a large bowl with a piece of crust on top.

Recipe Notes:
If you don't have fresh rabbit you can often find the frozen already cut and ready to cook

Feel free to substitute vegetables to match your taste and/or what you have on hand – the ones I choose are Nan's favorites

Don't skimp on the herbs, although it seems like a lot it really does make the dish – having said that this is another area you can adjust the recipe to your taste – pick one dominant herb and then go a little lighter with 2 4 others.

eat this with...

Ancient Peaks Merlot
Chateau margene Cabernet Franc
HammerSky Cabernet Franc
Halter Ranch Merlot
Hearst Ranch Malbec
Le Vigne Merlot
Pear Valley Malbec
Pretty-Smith Cabernet Franc
Silver Horse Malbec

chili

Chili was always the first thing I made when I was at my vacation condo in Utah. There is nothing like coming off the ski slopes and heading home for a big hot bowl of chili. I like mine loaded with vegetables and topped with cheese. I also tend to go a little spicy so adjust to suit your taste.

Serves 6-8

2 tablespoons olive oil
1 large onion, chopped
2 stalks celery, chopped
1 bell pepper, chopped
2 cups sliced button mushrooms
1 pound lean ground beef
1 can (28 ounces) diced tomatoes
1 can (28 ounces) red kidney beans

1 can (6 ounces) sliced black olives
1 jar (6 ounces) sliced hot jalapenos
4 tablespoons chili powder
1 teaspoon cayenne pepper
1 teaspoon cumin
1 tablespoon dried thyme
Salt, to taste
1 cup shredded sharp cheddar (optional)

- Heat olive oil in a large pot. Sauté onions, celery, bell peppers and mushrooms for 5 minutes.
- Add the ground beef to the pot and continue to stir until beef begins to brown.
- Add tomatoes, beans, olives, jalapenos, spices and salt. Stir and bring to a bowl. Reduce heat and allow to simmer for 3 hours.
- Serve topped with cheese.

eat this with...

Derby Zinfandel
Eberle Barbera
J&J Cellars Barbera
Niner Barbera
Pear Valley Syrah

beef mushroom barley soup

The rich broth, flavorful beef, chewy mushrooms and filling barley make this soup a complete meal.

Serves 6

1/2 ounce dried shiitake mushrooms	2 cups sliced fresh mushrooms
3 cups boiling water	4 cups beef broth
1 top sirloin steak (12 ounces)	1/4 cup soy sauce
1 tablespoon olive oil	1 tablespoon dried thyme
2 cloves garlic, minced	1/2 cup raw pearl barley
1 large onion, chopped	Salt & pepper to taste
2 stalks celery, chopped	
2 carrots, peeled and chopped	

- Place dried mushrooms in boiling water and simmer for 15 minutes. Remove from heat and allow to cool.
- Heat olive oil in a large pot. Brown the steak in the oil on both sides, remove from pot and season with salt and pepper.
- In the same oil used to brown the steak, sauté the garlic, onions, celery, carrots and mushrooms. Sauté until vegetables begin to soften and mushrooms begin to release their juices. Add beef broth, soy sauce, thyme and pearl barley to the pot.
- Drain the dried mushrooms, reserving the mushroom stock. Cut off and discard any tough stems, then rinse and chop the mushrooms. Add the mushrooms to the soup pot. Strain the mushroom stock through a sieve and add stock to the pot.
- Stir soup and bring to a boil, then place steak in the pot, reduce heat and cover. Simmer for 45 minutes.
- Remove steak and cut into 1/2 inch cubes. Return beef to the pot, stir and season with salt and pepper.
- Serve with warm bread.

eat this with...
Ancient Peaks Cabernet Sauvignon
Clavo Cellars Syrah
Eberle Syrah
Halter Ranch Cabernet Sauvignon
JUSTIN Cabernet Sauvignon
Still Waters Cabernet Sauvignon
Windward Pinot Noir

Chapter 5 - Soups, stews & chili

beef bourguignon

My beef bourguignon recipe follows techniques by Julia Child; however, is a healthier version with less fat and more vegetables. Let this simmer all afternoon and the wonderful aroma will fill the entire house.

eat this with...

AronHill Cabernet Sauvignon
Calcareous Cabernet Sauvignon
Caliza Cabernet Sauvignon
Chateau Margene Cabernet Sauvignon
Chumeia Cabernet Sauvignon
DAOU Cabernet Sauvignon
Eberle Cabernet Sauvignon
Hearst Ranch Cabernet Sauvignon
J. Lohr Cabernet Sauvignon
Nadeau Cabernet Sauvignon
Liberty School Cabernet Sauvignon
Penman Springs Cabernet Sauvignon
Pretty-Smith Cabernet Sauvignon
Ranchita Canyon Cabernet Sauvignon
Tobin James Cabernet Sauvignon

Chapter 5 - Soups, stews & chili

Serves 8

- 4 pound chuck roast, cut into 2-inch cubes)
- 2+1 tablespoons olive oil
- 2 tablespoons flour
- 1 teaspoon salt
- 1 teaspoon course ground pepper
- 1 teaspoon dried thyme
- 1 large onion sliced
- 2 cloves of garlic, finely chopped
- 1 bottle dry red wine
- 2 cups beef broth
- 1 tablespoon tomato paste
- 1 teaspoon dried sage
- 3 dried bay leaves
- 2 pounds mushrooms, quartered
- 2 medium turnips, peeled and cut into 1-inch cubes
- 4 carrots, peeled and cut into 1-inch pieces
- Salt & pepper, to taste
- Fresh parsley, chopped

∽ Preheat oven to 450F.

∽ Using a paper towel, dab beef pieces to remove moisture (this will make it easier to brown). Heat 2 tablespoons of oil in a large Dutch oven and over high heat brown beef pieces on all sides. Work in batches to give the beef plenty of room. As the beef is browned, remove it from the pan and to a large bowl. Coat the browned beef in flour, salt, pepper and thyme.

∽ Using the same pot, sauté the onions and garlic. When the onions start to soften, return the beef to the pot, remove from the stove top and place in oven, uncovered. After 5 minutes, remove from the oven and stir, return to the oven for an addition 5 minutes. This should form a light crust on the beef that will keep it moist and tender during the long cooking process. Remove from oven and reduce oven temperature to 325F.

∽ On the stove top, add the wine, beef stock, tomato paste, sage, bay leaves and stir. Once it reaches a slow boil, remove from stove top, place lid on the pot and return to the oven where it will slowly simmer for 3 hours.

∽ 45 minutes before the beef is ready, sauté the mushrooms in the remaining tablespoon of olive oil. Once they begin to release their juices, season with salt and pepper, and sauté for one additional minute.

∽ Add the mushrooms, turnips and carrots to the beef, stir and then place lid back on to continue to cook in the oven for the remaining 40 minutes. Prior to serving, taste and then season with additional salt and pepper as required. Serve in large bowls with a sprinkle of parsley for garnish.

Entrées

These wine friendly entrées range from simple dishes that can be prepared for a quick and easy meal, to those that may require some hunting for ingredients and plenty of preparation.

fish casserole - 107

grilled salmon - 108

fettuccini di mare - 109

macadamia nut crusted halibut - 111

halibut with green salsa - 112

lemon caper tilapia - 113

gary's paella - 115

duck paella with mushrooms - 116

duck breast with orange sauce - 118

herb roasted chicken - 119

cherry game hens - 121

lapin à la moutarde - 123

garlic stuffed pork roast - 124

pork chops with sautéed apples - 125

grilled chevon - 126

braised lamb shank - 127

rosemary lamb chops - 128

lamb kabobs - 129

ballistic zinfandel braised lamb shank - 131

eggplant bolognese - 132

spicy beef ribs - 133

fennel braised short ribs - 134

braised short ribs - 135

liver and onions - 136

blue cheese stuffed steak - 137

beef stroganoff - 138

flank steak with chimicurri sauce - 139

grillards de bœuf - 140

grilled elk steak - 142

grilled flank steak - 143

fish casserole

One of my favorite summer suppers is fish casserole. Loaded with flavor, yet very light, this dish is easy to make and goes well with a number of Paso Robles white wines. Don't skip the anchovies since they give the casserole a very nice, almost nutty flavor.

SERVES 4

3 tablespoons olive oil
2 ounce can of anchovies
1 tablespoon butter
1 ½ cups white wine
1.5 pounds white fish fillets (cod,
   tilapia or halibut work well)

3 large shallots, sliced
2 lemons, thinly sliced
3 tomatoes, thinly sliced
3 large basil leaves, chopped
Salt and pepper to taste

4 cups cooked basmati rice

- Pre-heat oven to 375F
- Heat olive oil in a casserole or skillet that can be used on both the stove top and in the oven. When the oil is hot add the anchovies, stirring until they dissolve. Add butter and stir until melted then add the wine, reduce the heat and simmer for 10 minutes.
- Remove from heat and add fish fillets. Arrange shallots, lemons and tomatoes over fish. Spoon some of the liquid from the bottom of the pan over all the ingredients. Add the fresh basil and season with salt and pepper.
- Bake in the oven for 30 minutes.
- Serve over rice. Be sure to spoon some of the juice over the top of each portion.

eat this with...

Caliza Grenache Blanc
Clayhouse Chenin Blanc
Eberle Chardonnay
Hearst Ranch Chardonnay
J. Lohr Chardonnay
L'Aventure Roussanne
Meridian Chardonnay
Tablas Creek Grenache Blanc
Tassajara Chardonnay
Tobin James Chardonnay
Wild Horse Chardonnay

grilled salmon

It is hard to go wrong with a beautiful, wild-caught salmon and a grill. Even the non-fish eaters tend to like a good grilled salmon every now and then.

eat this with...

Ancient Peaks Merlot
Falcon Nest Merlot
HammerSky Merlot
Kenneth Volk Merlot
Oso Libre Rosé
Rabbit Ridge Merlot
Robert Hall Rosé
Tablas Creek Rosé

Serves 4

1 large salmon fillet
1 lemon, juiced
3 lemons, thinly sliced
1 ounce fresh bay leaves
Olive oil for grill basket
Salt, to taste

Yogurt Dill Sauce

1 cup plain yogurt
2 tablespoons fresh dill, chopped
1 tablespoon capers
1 clove garlic, minced

- Mix together all ingredients. Best if made several hours to one day ahead to allow flavors to blend.

- Rub lemon juice into both sides of the salmon, sprinkle non-skin side with a little salt and arrange 3/4 of the sliced lemons and bay leaves on top.

- Oil a grill basket with olive oil and arrange the remaining lemons and bay leaves on the bottom of the basket then place the salmon in the basket and close.

- Grill over medium heat for 6-8 minutes per side. The goal is to cook the salmon until it is almost cooked through, then let the fish rest for 5 minutes and it will cook all the way through. Remove the bay leaves and some of the lemon slices prior to serving.

- Serve with Yogurt Dill Sauce on the side.

fettuccini di mare

A large bowl filled with pasta and shellfish in tomato sauce is a wonderful meal to serve any time of the year. Lobster is excellent in this dish as well...feel free to substitute your favorite items from the sea in this recipe.

Serves 4

1 tablespoon olive oil
8-12 large scallops
1 pound shrimp, (21-25 count) peeled
1 medium onion, diced
3 cloves garlic, minced
1 28 ounce can stewed tomatoes
1 cup dry white wine
1 tablespoon dried thyme
Salt and pepper to taste
8-12 littleneck clams, scrubbed
1/4 cup chopped fresh basil
6 cups fettuccini cooked al a dente

eat this with...

Anglim Rosé
AronHill Primitivo
Cass Grenache
Edward Sellers Grenache
Grey Wolf Rosé
Halter Ranch Grenache
Still Waters Rosé
Tobin James Primitivo
Zenaida Cellars Primitivo

- Heat olive oil in a large pan and sauté scallops and shrimp just long enough to give them a little color. Remove from pan.

- In the same pan, sauté onions and garlic for 3 minutes, add more oil if required.

- Add stewed tomatoes, wine, thyme, salt and pepper and bring to a boil. Reduce heat to simmer and place clams in pan, cover and allow to steam for approximately 5 minutes. The clams should all be open.

- Return scallops and shrimp to pan. Add basil and stir. Simmer for 5 more minutes.

- Place cooked fettuccini in large pasta bowls and top with sauce and seafood. Be sure to divide seafood evenly between the bowls.

macadamia nut crusted halibut
with coconut-papaya beurre blanc by Chef Ryan, Robert's Restaurant

Robert's Restaurant in down town Paso Robles is a plush dining room that features a modern approach to the American Classic theme, both in decor and menu. This halibut recipe is a good example; a fresh twist on a coastal favorite. Frequent Winery Dinner Events at Robert's showcase the talents of the area's winemakers, Executive Chef Ryan Swarthout and the team at Robert's Restaurant.

6 ounces Halibut
1 egg, beaten
¼ cup all purpose flour
¼ cup Macadamia nuts, finely chopped
¼ cup Panko Bread crumbs
2 tablespoons olive oil

Sauce

1 cup white wine
½ cup heavy cream
¼ pound butter, cubed
¼ cup papaya, diced
¼ cup shredded unsweetened coconut

- Place the halibut on a paper tower and pat dry. Place the flour, egg wash in separate bowls. Mix the macadamia nut and bread crumbs together and place in a separate bowl. Dredge the halibut in the flour, then the egg wash, then into the bread crumb-nut mixture. Set aside until ready to cook.
- Place the white wine in a sauce pot over medium high heat. Reduce the wine to ¼ cup and add the cream, continue cooking. Reduce the cream mixture by 2/3, remove from heat and slowly whisk the butter in. Once all the butter is added, season with salt and pepper. Add the papaya and shredded coconut to the wine sauce.
- Heat the 2 tablespoons of olive oil in a sauté pan over medium heat. Carefully add the halibut to the pan macadamia nut crust side down first. Cook for 2-3 minutes maybe longer depending on the thickness of the fish. Flip once and remove from the heat, let the heat from the pan finish cooking the halibut. Place the halibut on top of green onion rice pilaf, sautéed snow peas and drizzle the Coconut-Papaya Beurre Blanc on top of the fish and around the edge of the plate.

halibut with green salsa

Alaskan halibut and Chilean seabass are my two favorite kinds of fish. This recipe works equally well with either. The fish is moist and tender when cooked with the steam tent.

Serves 4

4 halibut medallions (about 6 ounces each)
1 teaspoon olive oil
Salt & pepper to taste

- ↝ Preheat oven to 350F
- ↝ Set halibut on a large sheet of foil paper, drizzle with oil and season with salt and pepper.
- ↝ Make a tent with the foil paper, leaving plenty of air space on top while forming a seal with the ends of the foil. Place on a baking sheet and bake until opaque (approximately 15 minutes).
- ↝ Serve with a spoonful of salsa on top.

Note: If you prefer a chopped tomato, basil and garlic salsa that also tastes great with the halibut.

Salsa

2 tablespoons olive oil
2 tablespoons chopped fresh parsley
1 tablespoon finely chopped shallots
1 tablespoon chopped capers
1 clove garlic, minced
1 tablespoon lemon fresh lemon juice
1/2 teaspoon anchovy paste (optional)
Salt & pepper, to taste

- ↝ **Combine all ingredients in a bowl and season with salt and pepper.**

eat this with...

Derby Pinot Gris
L'Aventure Viognier
Opolo Pinot Grigio
Pear Valley Chardonnay

lemon caper tilapia

Lemons, capers and fish are a combination you will see often. I use tilapia in this recipe; however, feel free to use your favorite meaty white fish such as monkfish or halibut.

Serves 4

8 small tilapia filets
2 tablespoons olive oil
1 lemon, sliced with seeds removed
3 tablespoons capers
Salt to taste

Marinade

1 cup dry white wine
Juice of two lemons
1 clove garlic, minced
1 tablespoon fresh basil

- Place fish in a nonmetallic container. Mix together marinade ingredients and pour over fish, seal the container and refrigerate. Marinate for 30 minutes.

- Heat olive oil in a frying pan or small wok. Reserve marinade and place fish in pan over medium heat. Cook on each side approximately 1 minute. Do not allow fish to cook all the way through. Remove fish from oil and add lemon slices, capers and reserved marinade. Allow mixture to reduce by half then return fish to the pan. Gently stir until fish is warm all the way through. Serve fish topped with lemon slices and capers.

eat this with...

Clavo Cellars Sauvignon Blanc
Eberle Pinto Grigio
Halter Ranch Sauvignon Blanc
Hearst Ranch Sauvignon Blanc
J. Lohr Riesling
JUSTIN Sauvignon Blanc
Le Vigne Pinto Grigio
Tobin James Sauvignon Blanc

gary's paella by Gary Eberle, Eberle Winery

Gary's Paella recipe is an Eberle favorite. Each year Gary makes this recipe for the holiday party and the entire staff can't wait to get a plate and dig in. Don't wait for the holidays to try this one.

Serves 10-12

1/4 cup olive oil
1/2 pound boneless chicken, cut into bite size pieces
1 large onion
1/4 cup water
2 cups uncooked rice
3 garlic cloves, chopped
24 ounces tomatoes, chopped plus juice from can (if using canned)
3 teaspoons salt
1/2 tablespoons chicken bouillon
1 tablespoon paprika

3/4 teaspoon pepper
1/4 teaspoon saffron
1/2-1 teaspoon crushed red pepper (to taste)
1 1/2 pounds shrimp, cleaned & deveined (tails are optional)
1 1/2 pounds sea scallops
1 1/2 pounds sausage—beef or pork
24 ounces artichoke hearts, quartered
16 ounces frozen peas
1 small jar pimientos or roasted red bell peppers
1 large can of large, pitted black olives
1 cup Cabernet Sauvignon

- Heat oil in large stock pot. Cook chicken in oil about 10 minutes and then remove from pan. Cook onion and garlic in oil until onion is transparent. Stir in water, wine, tomatoes, bouillon and all spices. Heat to boiling. Add chicken, shrimp, scallops and sausage. Simmer 15 minutes. Add more wine and water as needed.

- While other ingredients are cooking, cook 2 cups of rice in a separate pot. When cooked, drain and hold. Stir peas and artichoke hearts into first pot. Add about 3/4 of the rice and simmer for 5 minutes. If desired, add more rice for a drier dish. Serve in a paella dish or shallow baking dish. Garnish with pimentos or red bell peppers and black olives.

eat this with...

Eberle Cabernet Sauvignon

duck paella with mushrooms

by Maggie D'Ambrosia, Windward Vineyard

This is a classic dish that comes together in about an hour and doesn't require a special paella pan. Try this recipe from Windward when you want to impress your guests without spending hours in the kitchen. Heavenly when served with Windward Vineyard Pinot Noir.

Serves 6

1 cup dry white wine
1/2 teaspoon saffron threads
1 1/2 teaspoon sea salt
1 1/4 teaspoon smoked paprika
1 teaspoon freshly ground pepper
1 1/2 teaspoon dried thyme
2 tablespoons fresh parsley
2 cloves garlic, minced
2 1/2 pounds duck breast or legs
4 ounces sliced, fully cooked smoked
   Chorizo
1 tablespoon olive oil
1 1/2 cups chopped onion
3 cloves garlic, minced
1/2 pound mushrooms, cleaned &
   coarse chopped (porcini & baby
   bellas are perfect)
3 cups Arborio rice
5 1/2 cups low salt chicken broth
1-14 ounce can diced tomatoes in
   juice
2 red bell peppers, cut in 1/2" dice

Preheat oven to 400°F. Mix white wine & saffron threads in small measuring cup; set aside. Combine salt, smoked paprika, black pepper & herbs in small bowl; rub mixture all over duck. Heat heavy large ovenproof skillet over medium-high heat. Add chorizo and sauté until fat begins to render & sausage browns, stirring occasionally about 3 minutes. Transfer chorizo to large plate. Add olive oil to skillet. Add duck to skillet & cook until browned, about 4 minutes per side. Transfer to plate with chorizo.

Pour off all but 1 tablespoon of drippings from skillet. Reduce heat to medium. Add chopped onion and cook until translucent, stirring often. Add 4 cloves minced garlic & stir 30 seconds. Add mushrooms & sauté. Add rice & stir to coat. Add wine-saffron mixture & bring to boil, scraping up browned bits from bottom of skillet.

Add chicken broth, tomatoes with juice, and red peppers. Bring to simmer. Stir in browned chorizo. Place duck atop mixture in skillet (if using breasts, do not add until last 10 minutes of baking for medium-rare). Bake paella uncovered until rice is almost tender, about 20 minutes.

Transfer duck to plate. Stir rice; season to taste with salt & pepper. Return duck to skillet, nestling into rice. Bake until rice is tender, 5-10 minutes longer if necessary.

eat this with...
Windward Vineyard Estate Pinot Noir GOLD Barrel Select

Paso Pinot & Paella, an Annual Event

Marc Goldberg & Maggie D'Ambrosia were searching to create a wine & food pairing event that was different from the usual winemaker sit-down dinner format. The event needed to be a unique way of showcasing the diversity of Pinot Noir with a wide range of food and flavors. With a little help from Tom Fundaro from Villa Creek and Lynn Diehl of Wine Region News the First Pinot & Paella Event, in 2004, attracted 125 guests at Windward Vineyard. Paella was selected since there are virtually 450 different types of Paella: from seafood, to duck, lamb, vegetarian, basically incorporating any locally available ingredient with short grain rice and cooking on an open fire.

The event now features 20 Paso Pinot Noirs, 20 outstanding chefs creating 20 different paellas, live music under the shade of Big Oaks in the beautiful Templeton Park with live music & dancing. Attendance is limited to 500 guests in order to emphasize the quality and not quantity and 100% of the proceeds benefit local youth arts foundations. Visit www.pinotandpaella.com for additional information.

duck breast with orange sauce

Duck is my favorite item to order when dining in Paris. I have found American duck is also pretty darn good. Be sure not to overcook since duck breast meat is best rare to medium-rare.

- Place duck breasts in a glass container and pour marinade ingredients over top. Cover container, shake to coat breasts and marinate for 45 minutes. Remove breasts from container reserving marinade.

- Using a sharp knife, score the skin of the duck breasts diagonally to create 3/4 inch-wide diamond pattern; pat dry then season with salt and pepper. Heat a heavy skillet over high heat. Place duck breasts in skillet skin side down and cook until skin is a deep golden brown -- about 8 minutes. Turn duck over; cook about 3 minutes for medium-rare. Transfer breasts to baking sheet and place in oven pre-heated to 250F to keep warm.

- Pour all but 2 tablespoons of the drippings from the skillet. With heat set to medium high, pour Triple Sec or brandy into pan and scrap up the browned bits. Pour reserved marinade into pan and bring to a full boil for 2 minutes stirring occasionally. Add sage, salt and pepper. Reduce heat to low and allow to simmer until juices are reduced by half.

- Slice duck breasts and drizzle with orange sauce prior to serving.

Serves 2

2 duck breasts
1/4 cup Triple Sec orange liqueur
1 teaspoon dried sage
Salt and pepper, to taste

Marinade

1 cup fresh squeezed orange juice
1/4 cup soy sauce
1 tablespoon orange zest
Juice of one lemon

eat this with...
Anglim Syrah
Eos Gewurztraminer
Pear Valley Syrah

herb roasted chicken

Every now and then on a Sunday evening I like to cook the kind of meals my family ate when I was a little girl. Sundays were typically roast beef, roasted chicken or ham. Roasted chicken with simple dry herbs is comfort food that all of my friends enjoy. Be sure to serve with mashed potatoes.

Serves 6

5 pound chicken
2 tablespoons of olive oil
1 tablespoon dried thyme
½ tablespoon dried sage
Salt and pepper to taste
2 cups of chicken stock
1 onion chopped

eat this with...
Adelaida Cellars Chardonnay
J. Lohr Rosé
L'Aventure Rosé
Terry Hoage Bam Bam

- Preheat oven to 375F.

- Wash chicken and pat dry. Rub olive oil on chicken then sprinkle with herbs, salt and pepper.

- Pour chicken stock in the bottom of a roasting pan large enough to fit the chicken with plenty of room for the chicken to brown. Add the chopped onion to the chicken stock, place chicken in pan and insert into preheated oven.

- Cook chicken for 1 – 1.5 hours, basting every 20 minutes. The chicken should be removed from the oven when it reaches 160F (it is best to stick the thermometer in the center of the thigh to test). Let the chicken rest for 10 minutes prior to carving -- the chicken should then reach a temperature of 170F and be nice and juicy.

cherry game hens

Game hens cut in half, marinated and grilled are awesome all on their own. Add this cherry wine sauce and you have a gourmet delight. The sauce is also excellent on chicken and pork.

Serves 4

2 Cornish game hens, cut in half lengthwise

Marinade

1/2 cup olive oil
1/4 cup Balsamic vinegar
1/4 cup soy sauce
1 teaspoon dried sage
1 teaspoon dried thyme

Sauce

1 cup dried cherries
2 cups Port of fruity red wine
1 tablespoon brown sugar
2 tablespoons Balsamic vinegar

- Place hens in a container for marinating. Mix together marinade ingredients and pour over hens. Marinate for 2-3 hours in a sealed, refrigerated container.

- Stir all sauce ingredients together and bring to a boil. Reduce heat and allow to simmer until sauce reduces to half its volume.

- While the sauce is simmering, grill hens over medium heat until cooked through, approximately 8 minutes per side.

- Allow hens to rest for 5-10 minutes, Serve with a generous portion of cherry sauce poured on top.

eat this with...

Caliza Petite Sirah
Cass Petite Sirah
Cypher Zinfandel
DAOU Petite Sirah
Eberle Barbera
Epoch Zinfandel
Jack Creek Cellars Syrah
J&J Cellars Autumn Flight Barbera
Hearthstone Syrah
Pear Valley Syrah
Rabbit Ridge Petite Sirah
Tobin James "Bella Bella" Barbera
Venteux Petite Sirah
Zenaida Zinfandel
Zin Alley Zinfandel

lapin à la moutarde

This rabbit with mustard sauce will impress your friends. Although rabbit was once considered peasant food, it is now considered a delicacy. Save any leftover mustard sauce to serve with pork, chicken or fish.

SERVES 4

2 cups red wine
¼ cup olive oil
1 teaspoon sage
1 teaspoon marjoram
2 tablespoons Worcestershire sauce
2 tablespoons soy sauce
2 pounds of rabbit pieces

Mustard Sauce

1 tablespoon butter
2 scallions, finely chopped
¼ cup Dijon mustard
¼ cup stone ground mustard
1 cup red wine
1 teaspoon thyme
1 tablespoon brown sugar
Salt and pepper to taste
¼ cup fresh parsley, chopped

- Mix one cup of red wine, olive oil, sage, marjoram, Worcestershire sauce and soy sauce together to create marinade. Place rabbit pieces in a non-metallic container or zip lock bag and pour the marinade over rabbit. Seal the container and place in refrigerator to marinate for 4 hours.

- In a sauce pan, melt butter and sauté scallions on medium heat for approximately 5 minutes. Stir in mustard, wine, thyme, sugar and bring to a boil. Reduce heat and simmer until sauce reduces by half then add salt and pepper to taste.

- Grill rabbit pieces on medium heat for approximately 5 minutes per side. When rabbit is cooked remove from grill and let rest for 5 minutes.

- While the rabbit rests, stir the parsley into the warm sauce, reserving a little for garnish. When ready to serve, pour a generous portion of sauce over the rabbit. Garnish with reserved parsley.

eat this with...

Ancient Peaks Merlot
DAOU Grenache Blanc
Edward Sellers Grenache
Graveyard Tombstone Pink
Pear Valley Merlot
Pretty-Smith Palette de Rouge
Ranchita Canyon Petit Verdot
San Marcos Creek Chardonnay
Tablas Creek Esprit De Beaucastel Blanc
Tobin James Merlot
Terry Hoage Bam Bam

garlic stuffed pork roast

Garlic and pork are a winning flavor combination. The cloves roasted in the pork make a pretty presentation when the meat is sliced. Very wine friendly, so visit chapter 10 and pick a wine.

Serves 6

4-5 pound pork loin roast
4 cloves garlic, peeled and sliced
Salt and pepper to taste

- Preheat oven to 375F.

- Using a sharp knife make small incisions all around the roast. Insert garlic slices into incisions and then place pork in roasting pan. Pour enough sauce over the roast so that the bottom of the pan is covered in liquid (approximately half of the marinade) Season with salt and pepper to taste then roast for approximately 90 minutes (internal temperature should be 150F).Baste roast with liquids every 30 minutes.

- Let roast rest for 10 minutes before carving.

Sauce

1 cup dry white wine
1/4 cup olive oil
1/4 cup lemon juice
1 tablespoon dried rosemary
1/2 tablespoon dried thyme

- Mix all ingredients together.

eat this with...
Doce Robles Merlot
Halter Ranch Malbec
Pear Valley Distraction
Penman Springs Merlot
Pretty-Smith Palette de Rouge

pork chops with sautéed apples

Apples are not just for dessert. Try them on pork chops.

Serves 4

1 tablespoon ginger paste
1 tablespoon soy sauce
4 thick pork chops

Sautéed Apples

2 apples sliced
2 tablespoons lemon juice
2 tablespoons apple juice
1 tablespoon each - butter and olive oil
1 teaspoon each - ground cloves and ginger
1 tablespoon brown sugar

- Mix ginger paste and sou sauce and rub on both sides of pork chops.

- Melt olive oil and butter in a large skillet. Sauté apple slices in oil/butter mixture for 3-5 minutes. Reduce heat to low and add juice, cloves, ginger and brown sugar. Gently heat for 10 more minutes stirring frequently.

- While the apples are cooking, grill the pork chops for approximately 5 minutes per side.

- Serve pork chops with sautéed apples on top.

eat this with...

Calcareous Chardonnay
Castoro Cellars Gewurztraminer
Chronic Cellars Riesling
Meridian Gewurztraminer

grilled chevon

Yes, it is goat meat and it tastes great. One of my friend's family has a goat ranch not far from my vineyard and when she said the butcher had just prepared a package and offered me some chops I wasn't going to turn them down. The goats from the Miller Moth Ranch always produce tender, flavorful meat. Most of my experience with goat meat was in Jamaica where they tend to do a lot of curry and jerk dishes. I decided to go with a light marinade and grill to let the goat flavor shine through.

Serves 4

4 chevon chops
Salt & pepper, to taste

Marinade

1 cup white wine
1/4 cup olive oil
1 clove garlic, minced
2 teaspoons dried thyme

- Place chops in ziplock bag. Mix together marinade ingredients together and pour over chops. Seal bag and marinate in refrigerator for 2 hours.

- Remove chops for marinade, season with salt and pepper then grill for approximately 4 minutes per side. Let the chops rest for 5 minutes prior to serving.

eat this with...

Eberle Côtes-du-Rôbles Blanc
Edward Sellers Roussanne
Le Cuvier Rosé
Pretty-Smith Palette de Rouge
Venteux Roussanne

braised lamb shank

When you can find good lamb shanks, there is nothing like braising with loads of rosemary.

Serves 2

2 lamb shanks
1 tablespoon all purpose flour
Salt & pepper, to taste
2 tablespoons olive oil
1 onion, chopped
2 cloves of garlic, minced
4 tablespoons fresh rosemary, chopped
3 cups red wine
2 tablespoons tomato paste

- Preheat oven to 375F.

- Sprinkle flour, salt and pepper on lamb shanks.

- In a medium sized Dutch oven, heat olive oil. Saute onions and garlic for 2 minutes. Add lamb shanks and brown on both sides over high heat. Remove shanks and add rosemary, red wine and tomato paste. Stir and bring to a boil. Return shanks to the Dutch oven, cover and place in preheated oven and cook for 3 hours.

eat this with...

Adelaida Cellars Cabernet Franc
Derby Cabernet Franc
Falcon Nest Cabernet Sauvignon
Graveyard Syrah
J. Dusi Syrah
Jada Syrah
L'Aventure Optimus
Pretty-Smith Cabernet Franc
Tablas Creek Esprit de Beaucastel
Vina Robles Cabernet Sauvignon

rosemary lamb chops

Lamb chops are perfect when you want a quick but elegant meal for entertaining.

Serves 4

8 lamb chops
1 teaspoon, olive oil
2 tablespoons fresh rosemary, chopped
Salt & pepper, to taste
4 sprigs fresh rosemary

- ⌁ Coat chops in oil, rosemary, salt and pepper.

- ⌁ Grill on high heat for 2 minutes on each side to give chops a good sear. Reduce grill heat and grill an additional 2-3 minutes on each side.

- ⌁ Serve garnished with a sprig of rosemary.

eat this with...
Bodegas Paso Robles Iberia
Pear Valley Distraction
Pretty-Smith Cabernet Franc

lamb kabobs

You could use lamb stewing meat for this but I tend to go with a high quality cut. Either way the lamb tastes great grilled.

Serves 4

1.5 pounds lamb cut into 1 inch cubes
2 red bell peppers cut into 1 inch squares
1 yellow onion cut into 1 inch squares
Salt and pepper to taste

Marinade

1/2 cup lemon juice
1/4 olive oil
1/4 cup honey
1/4 cup fresh mint, chopped
1 teaspoon dried rosemary

- Place lamb cubes in a ziplock bag, mix together marinade ingredients and pour over lamb. Seal the bag, shake and marinate in the refrigerator for 2 hours.
- Skewer lamb, onion and bell pepper then season with salt and pepper to taste.
- Grill for approximately 5 minutes on each side.

eat this with...

Cass Grenache
HammerSky Cabernet Franc
Le Vigne Cabernet Franc
Pear Valley Merlot
Robert Hall Cabernet Franc
Vina Robles Signature
Wild Horse Merlot

ballistic zinfandel braised lamb shank

by Chef Marc LeDuc, Tobin James Cellars

Try an incredibly delicious Tobin James favorite.
This is an easy, succulent dish that you can prepare any time, any season!

Serves 2

- 2 lamb shanks
- 1 cup celery, chopped
- 1 cup carrot, chopped
- 2 cups sweet yellow onion, chopped
- 2 cups Ballistic Zinfandel
- 4 garlic cloves

- 8 sprigs fresh thyme
- 3 fresh bay leaves
- 4 cups lamb or beef stock
- 30 ounces organic tomato sauce
- 4-8 cups water
- Salt and pepper to taste
- 2 tablespoons grape seed oil

- Season the lamb shanks with salt and pepper, then using a dutch oven brown them in the hot grape seed oil.
- Add the celery, onion and carrot and sweat until soft.
- Add the herbs then the wine and simmer until the wine is almost evaporated.
- Add the stock, tomato sauce and water; bring to a simmer and cook until meat is tender about 3 hours.
- Pull out the shanks and plate.
- Strain the sauce off all the vegetables and herbs and use as a sauce.
- If the sauce is too thick during the cooking process use more stock to thin. If the sauce is too thin after cooking is done let it simmer until desired thickness.

eat this with...

Tobin James Ballistic Zinfandel
Tobin James Dusi Vineyard Zinfandel
Tobin James "James Gang" Reserve Zinfandel
Tobin James Silver Reserve Zinfandel
Tobin James French Camp Vineyards Zinfandel
Tobin James Blue Moon Reserve Zinfandel

eggplant bolognese

Bolognese is a meat-based sauce typically used for pasta that originated in Bologna Italy. The sauce can be made a few different ways but always tends to have meat, onions, garlic and a small amount of tomatoes. Some recipes call for milk to bring out the flavor of the meat; however, I use wine in mine to help with pairing it with a glass with the meal.

Serves 6

1 eggplant
1 tablespoon olive oil
Salt to taste

¼ cup freshly grated Pecorino Romano

eat this with...

Caliza Mourvedre
Epoch Tempranillo
Grey Wolf Mourvedre
Locatelli Malbec
Opolo Merlot
Riverstar Merlot
Tobin James Malbec
Victor Hugo Malbec

Sauce

2 tablespoons olive oil
1 onion, chopped
3 cloves garlic, finely chopped
1 pound lean ground beef
1 28-ounce can diced tomatoes
1 cup dry red wine
5 basil leaves, chopped
4 tablespoons fresh parsley, chopped
Salt & pepper to taste

- Preheat oven to 400F.

- In a large saucepan heat the olive oil and sauté the onions and garlic. When onion becomes translucent add the ground beef and continue to stir until the meat is lightly browned. Stir in the tomatoes, wine, basil, parsley, salt and pepper. Bring to a boil and then reduce the heat to simmer. Allow the sauce to simmer for at least 30 minutes so the flavors blend and the sauce thickens.

- While the sauce is simmering slice the eggplant (if the eggplant is bitter salt and let rest for 20 minutes then rinse and pat dry). Lightly coat the eggplant in olive oil and sprinkle with a little salt. Roast in oven heated to 400F for 20 minutes, turning after 10 minutes.

- Spoon enough of the sauce to cover the bottom of a baking dish, then add roasted eggplant, then more sauce. Repeat the layers until all eggplant and sauce have been used then sprinkle the top with grated Pecorino Romano. Place in the oven until the cheese is melted and golden brown.

spicy beef ribs

These spicy ribs are slow cooked until the meat is tender and falling off the bone.

Serves 6

3 pounds beef short ribs
1/2 teaspoon salt
1/4 teaspoon pepper
1/2 cup flour
2 tablespoons olive oil
2 cloves of garlic, crushed
1 small onion, chopped
2 stalks celery, chopped
28 ounce can stewed tomatoes
2 cups dry red wine
1 tablespoon Worcestershire sauce
1 teaspoon cayenne pepper
1/2 teaspoon thyme
1/2 teaspoon marjoram
Juice of one lemon

- Combine salt, pepper and flour. Dredge meat in flour mixture.
- Heat olive oil in a large pan. Brown meat in oil on both sides. Remove meat, sauté garlic, onions and celery for 3 minutes, adding additional olive oil if required to prevent vegetables from sticking. Stir in remaining ingredients reserving lemon juice. Bring to a boil, return meat to the pan, reduce heat to simmer and cover. Simmer for 2 1/2 hours or until meat is very tender.
- Add lemon juice and simmer for 10 more minutes.

eat this with...

Castoro Petite Sirah
Eberle Barbara
Eos Petite Sirah
Niner Barbera
Ranchita Canyon Old Vine Petite Sirah
Vina Robles Petite Sirah
Vista Del Rey Barbera

fennel braised short ribs

Fennel adds a nice flavor to the braised short ribs. The vegetables and juice are fabulous spooned over steamed rice or mashed potatoes.

Serves 4

1.5 pounds boneless short ribs
1 cup dry red wine
2 fennel bulbs, thinly sliced
4 celery stalks, chopped
4 carrots, peeled and chopped
1/2 teaspoon dried sage
Salt & pepper, to taste

- Preheat oven to 375F.

- Place the ribs in a medium sized roasting pot along with fennel bulbs and celery. Pour wine over ribs and vegetables then sprinkle with sage, salt and pepper.

- Roast in oven for 30 minutes then baste juice over ribs. If they appear to be a little dry turn ribs over prior to placing back in oven. After an additional 30 minutes, add carrots to the roasting pan and once again baste ribs. Remove from oven when carrots are tender (approximately 20 minutes).

eat this with...

Calcareous Meritage
Chateau Margene Cabernet Sauvignon
DAOU Cabernet Sauvignon
Derby Cabernet Sauvignon
HammerSky Merlot
JUSTIN Malbec
Kenneth Volk Aglianico
Pear Valley Our Daily Red
Pretty-Smith Cabernet Sauvignon
Robert Hall Merlot
Silver Horse Tempranillo
Summerwood Merlot
Tobin James Merlot
Victor Hugo Malbec

braised short ribs

Braised short ribs pair well with so many of the red Paso Robles wines. The "eat this with..." box is too small to list them all, so be sure to look in Chapter 10 for other great wines.

Serves 4

2 tablespoons oil
1 onion, chopped
2 cloves garlic, minced
1.5 pounds boneless short ribs
2 cups dry red wine
1 cup beef stock
1 tablespoon tomato paste
2 teaspoons dried thyme
1 teaspoon dried chili flakes
Salt & pepper, to taste
2 carrots, chopped
2 parsnips, chopped

- Preheat oven to 375F.

- In a medium Dutch oven, heat oil and sauté onions and garlic for 5 minutes. Add ribs and brown on both sides. Add wine, stock, paste, thyme, chili flakes, salt and pepper. Bring to a boil and then add carrots and parsnips.

- Cover and roast in oven for 3 hours.

eat this with...

Clayhouse Petite Sirah
Doce Robles Barbera
Graveyard Dark Phathom
L'Aventure Optimus
Orchid Hill Petite Sirah
Ranchita Canyon Sangiovese
Steinbeck Mourvedre

liver and onions

Believe it or not, liver and onions served with mashed potatoes and peas is one of my favorite meals. I only use high quality liver from young animals.

Serves 4

1/4 cup all purpose flour
Salt & pepper, to taste
1 tablespoon olive oil
1 tablespoon butter
6 slices calf's liver, sliced 1/2 inch thick
1 large onion, sliced
2 tablespoons brandy

- Mix flour, salt and pepper. Dredge liver is flour mixture.

- Heat oil and butter in a medium frying pan. Quickly brown liver on each side and remove from the pan. Take care not to cook liver all the way through.

- Using the same pan, saute the onions for 3 minutes. Add brandy and cook for 3 more minutes. Return liver to the pan and cook for 1-2 minutes.

eat this with...

Halter Ranch Rosé
J. Lohr Rosé
J&J Cellars Rosé
L'Aventrue Rosé
Le Cuvier Rosé
Penman Springs Two Roses
Tablas Creek Rosé
Terry Hoage Bam Bam

blue cheese stuffed steak

While I am certain this recipe will work with a large number of wines, I created it specifically to go with Zinfandel. If you look in Chapter 10 you will find it is the varietal produced by the largest number of Paso Robles wineries. I haven't tried every Paso Zinfandel, but expect most will pair well with this recipe.

Serves 4

4 steaks (a thick cut of premium beef without bone works best)
4 tablespoons crumbled blue cheese
Salt & pepper to taste
1 cup of Zinfandel
¼ cup balsamic vinegar
½ teaspoon thyme
¼ teaspoon cayenne pepper
2 ounce bittersweet chocolate

- To make the sauce, add Zinfandel, vinegar, thyme and cayenne pepper to a sauce pan. Stir and bring to a full boil. Reduce heat and simmer until liquid reduces by half then stir in chocolate. Continue to stir until chocolate melts then remove from heat.

- While the sauce is simmering, using a sharp knife cut a pocket into the center of the steak. Using a spoon, stuff the pocket with blue cheese crumbles being careful to insert cheese far enough that it will not drip out when grilling. Season to taste with salt and pepper prior to grilling for 4-6 minutes per side for medium rare, or longer if desired. Remove from grill and let steak rest for 5 minutes. Drizzle with chocolate sauce prior to serving.

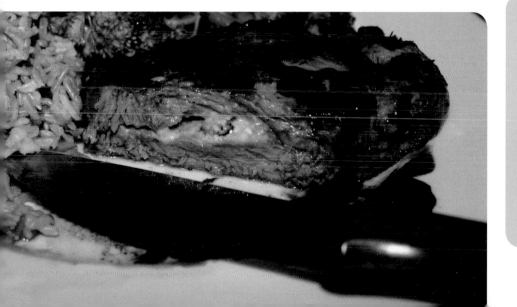

eat this with...

Adelaida Zinfandel
Cypher Zinfandel
Eos Zinfandel
Epoch Zinfandel
J. Dusi Zinfandel
Norman Zinfandel
Peachy Canyon Zinfandel
Penman Springs Zinfandel
San Marcos Creek Zinfandel
Tobin James Fatboy Zinfandel
Zin Alley Zinfandel

beef stroganoff

Beef stroganoff can be a little tricky to pair with wine. While you may think a Cabernet Sauvignon for the beef, chance are the cream sauce will make that seem very tannic and bitter. It is better with a nice, round white or a fruit forward light to medium bodied red.

Serves 4

1/4 cup butter (1/2 stick)
1.5 pounds sirloin, sliced thin
1 small onion, chopped
1 pound mushrooms, sliced
1 teaspoon dried tarragon
Salt & pepper, to taste
1 cup sour cream (at room temperature)
4 cups cooked egg noodles
1 tablespoon fresh tarragon, chopped

eat this with...

Asuncion Ridge Pinot Noir
Calcareous Chardonnay
Jack Creek Pinot Noir
J. Lohr Chardonnay
Orchid Hill Pinot Noir
Pear Valley Merlot
Tassajara Pinot Noir
Wild Horse Unbridled Merlot
Windward Vineyard Pinot Noir

- In a large frying pan melt butter. Brown meat slices on both sides and remove from pan.

- Using the same pan, saute onions and mushrooms. When the mushrooms begin to release their juice stir in dried tarragon, sat and pepper. Saute for approximately 4 minutes.

- Return meat to the pan, reduce heat and stir in sour cream. Do not allow the cream to simmer or boil, cook for just a couple of minutes.

- Serve immediately over egg noddles, garnished with fresh tarragon.

flank steak with chimicurri sauce

Chimicurri is not only fun to say but also tasty to eat, especially when served with Flank Steak.

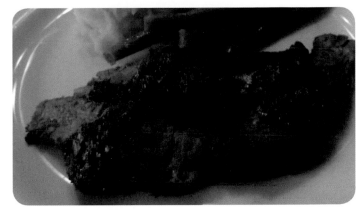

Serves 4

1.5 pound Flank Steak
1 cup dry red wine
¼ cup olive oil
1 teaspoon dried thyme
Salt & pepper to taste

- Place steak in a large ziplock bag. Mix wine, oil and thyme together and pour over steak. Be sure to coat entire steak, remove air and seal the bag then place in refrigerator to marinate for 2 hours.

- Remove steak from marinade and season with salt and pepper. Place on grill set to high heat and grill approximately 4 minutes per side. The steak is best when served rare to medium rare so be careful not to overcook. Remove from grill, cover with foil paper and let rest for 5-10 minutes.

- Make very thin slices, against the grain, and at a slight diagonal so that the slices are wide. Serve topped with Chimichurri Sauce.

Chimichurri Sauce

½ cup olive oil
1 cup fresh parsley
1 cup fresh cilantro
3 cloves of garlic
½ teaspoon cumin
1 teaspoon chili sauce
Juice of one lime
½ teaspoon salt

- Blend all ingredients together in a food processor. Make this at least 3 hours in advance so the flavors have time to blend together.

eat this with...

Edward Sellers Grenache
Hearst Ranch Malbec
Silver Horse Malbec
Tablas Creek Grenache

grillards de bœuf by Chef Jacob, Cass Winery

Locally raised, grass-fed, grilled beef flat-iron steaks, topped with seared duck foie gras & wine smoked mushrooms, sautéed chard & pommes dauphinoises. This course involves several different steps, each is broken down individually, and assembled afterwards.

For the Steaks:

> 4 4-6oz grass-fed flat-iron steaks
> Extra virgin olive oil
> Kosher or sea salt
> Freshly cracked pepper

Rub lightly with the olive oil. Apply the salt and pepper just minutes before cooking. Grill over your favorite wood. I would suggest cooking your steaks to a rare or medium-rare doneness. Let your steaks rest before serving.

Wine-soaked mushrooms:

> 1 pound of mushrooms (your choice here)
> 1 bottle Cass Winery Syrah
> ½ fresh rosemary sprig (2 or 3 inches worth)
> ½ cup beef demi-glace (available at finer food stores)
> Cracked pepper to taste
> Kosher salt to taste

eat this with...

Cass Edge, *a blend of Cabernet Sauvignon, Cabernet Franc, Merlot, Petit Verdot and Malbec*

Take the tip off of the mushrooms and save for your stock pot. Cut the mushrooms into quarters. Soak them in a glass bowl in the wine overnight. Put the entire contents of the bowl into a medium saucepan and cook over medium heat until all of the alcohol has burned off and the liquid has reduced by half. Add the remainder of the ingredients and simmer on low for approximately 15 minutes, or until mushrooms are tender and begin to 'give' when chewing. Remove the rosemary sprig before ladling.

Seared duck foie gras:

4 slices grade 'A' Sonoma Saveurs Moulard
duck foie gras, ¾ inch thick
Kosher salt
Cracked pepper
1 teaspoon butter
1 teaspoon vegetable oil

Heat the oil and butter together in a medium frying pan on high. Get the pan extremely hot, but not quite smoking. Lightly season the foie gras with salt and pepper. Fry the foie gras for approximately 45 seconds per side. Just until they begin to render and brown. Remove from the pan and serve immediately.

Pommes Dauphinoise:

1 ½ pounds slightly waxy potatoes
1 ½ cups milk
1 cup cream
1 clove garlic, thinly sliced

1 sprig fresh thyme
1 bay leaf
½ cup gruyère cheese, grated
Sea salt and freshly ground black pepper

Peel the potatoes and slice to the thickness of about a ½ dollar coin. In a large saucepan, bring the milk and cream to the boil. Add the garlic slivers, the thyme, bay and seasoning. Simmer 2 minutes then slide in the potatoes. Simmer for 5-7 minutes until the slices are soft but still whole. Drain in a colander set over a bowl to catch the creamy liquid. Remove the herb sprigs. Spoon the potatoes evenly into a gratin dish, sprinkling in between with two thirds of the cheese. Pour back the creamy milk until it just reaches the top of the potatoes. Top with the remaining cheese. Set aside in the fridge to chill until ready to bake. Heat the oven to 425 degrees. Bake for 15 minutes until golden brown and bubbling. Allow to stand for 10 minutes before serving.

Sauteed chard:

1 1//2 pounds rainbow chard, leaves and
tender stalk chopped coarsely
1 tablespoon unsalted butter
Sea salt to taste
Pepper to taste

In a medium size frying pan, melt the butter over medium heat. Add the chard and saute lightly until wilted, stirring several times. Season to taste. Drain off excess liquid before plating.

Plating: Start by gently punching out rings of pommes dauphinoise using a ring-mold, cookie cutter, etc. Using a spatula, transfer these the center of each plate. Top this with a mound of the sauteed chard (try to keep it all on the potatoes). Place a steak squarely atop each pile of chard and press lightly to secure. Top with the foie gras and the mushrooms in demi-glace. Garnish with fresh snipped chives.

grilled elk steak

Elk is very lean and loaded with flavor. I find marinating is the best way to ensure a tender steak.

Serves 4

1.5 pounds elk steaks
Salt & pepper, to taste

Marinade

1 cup red wine
1/4 cup olive oil
1 tablespoon Worcestershire sauce
2 cloves garlic, minced
1/2 teaspoon dried marjoram
1/2 teaspoon cayenne pepper

- Place elk in a ziplock bag. Mix marinade ingredients together and pour over steaks. Seal bag and marinate in refrigerator for 4 hours.
- Remove steaks from marinade and season with salt and pepper.
- Grill on high heat for 3-4 minutes per side.

eat this with...

Ancient Peaks Malbec
Caliza Petite Sirah
HammerSky Petit Verdot
Kenneth Volk Negrette
Oso Libre Grenache
Peachy Canyon Malbec
Pomar Junction Pinot Noir
Ranchita Canyon Petit Verdot
Silver Horse Malbec
Tobin James Refosco

grilled flank steak
with Shaved Parmesan Cheese and Arugula
by Niels & Bimmer Udsen, Castoro Cellars

Niels and Bimmer fell in love with the lime marinade in Brazil.
This recipe is their "Italy meets Brazil" version of grilled flank steak.

eat this with...

Castoro Cellars Primitivo
Castoro Cellars Zinfusion

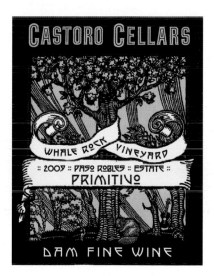

Serves 4

2 - 2 1/2 pound flank steaks
2-3 limes, juiced (enough juice to cover both sides of the meat)
Sea Salt coarse ground, to taste
1 cup arugula, chopped into 2 inch pieces
1/2 cup imported parmesan, shaved

- Drizzle lime juice over the meat and generously salt. Do both sides and let sit for an hour or so.

- Grill steaks on high heat to medium rare. Let rest 10 minutes.

- Cut thinly across the grain, layer on serving tray with arugula and parmesan cheese.

- Drizzle with a fresh local olive oil.

Sides

Here are a few vegetable, rice and pasta dishes that are great along with several of the entrée or small plate recipes found in earlier chapters. Since the wine is typically paired with the main element in the meal, "eat this with..." recommendations have not been included.

summer squash

If you have a vegetable garden there is always that point in the summer when it is difficult to keep up with the squash plants. I make this often when the squash are abundant.

Serves 6
> 3 small zucchini, cut in half moons
> 3 small yellow summer squash, cut in half moons
> 1 medium onion, chopped
> 2 tablespoon olive oil
> 2 tablespoons chopped cilantro
> Salt and pepper to taste

- Place a large piece of foil paper on the counter and mix all ingredients in the center. Wrap foil around squash mixture to create a sealed package.

- Place on grill at medium heat fro 10-15 minutes.

stir fried vegetables

Vegetables maintain their natural, good flavors when stir fried for a short amount of time with just a little oil and spice.

Serves 4

 1 tablespoon olive oil
 1 teaspoon sesame oil
 1 clove garlic, minced
 1 cup snow peas, tips cut off
 2 red bell peppers, seeded and sliced
 2 tablespoons soy sauce
 1 teaspoon Sriracha hot sauce
 1 cup pea sprouts

- Heat oil in a wok. Saute garlic for 1 minute then add in peas and peppers.

- Stir fry for 5 minutes then add soy and hot sauce. Stir an additional minute then add in pea sprouts, reserving a few sprouts for garnish.

- Serve garnished with raw sprouts.

roasted root vegetables

As vegetables roast their flavors become more enhanced. In the winter when root vegetables are readily available I often roast a large batch and have them all week long.

Serves 6

    4 red beets, peeled and chopped
    3 yellow beets, peeled and chopped
    1 large turnip, peeled and chopped
    2 parsnips, peeled and chopped
    3 carrots, peeled and chopped
    10 cloves of garlic, peeled
    6 sprigs of thyme
    3 tablespoon olive oil
    Salt & pepper to taste

- Preheat oven to 400F.
- Place all ingredients in a large roasting pan and stir to coat.
- Roast for 45 minutes, stirring occasionally.
- Remove thyme stems and serve hot, at room temperature or cold in a salad.

grilled vegetables

In Paso Robles, most of us do a lot of grilling. If the grill is fired up anyway, you might as well throw on a batch of vegetables. I use any fresh vegetables I have for this recipe.

Vegetables
- **4 heads baby bok choy**
- **1 green and 1 red bell pepper, seeded and cut into thick wedges**
- **1 large sweet onion, cut into large rings**
- **1 bundle asparagus**
- **8 baby bellas mushrooms, de-stemmed**

Marinade
- **1/2 cup olive oil**
- **1/4 cup soy sauce**
- **1/2 cup dry red wine**
- **3 cloves garlic, minced**
- **1 tablespoon celery seed**
- **1 tablespoon chopped fresh basil**
- **1 tablespoon chopped fresh oregano**

- Place all vegetables in a large glass container with a tight fitting lid.
- Mix together marinade ingredients and pour over vegetables and stir. Cover and marinate for 30-60 minutes.
- Grill over medium flame in a vegetable basket or BBQ meshed plate for 8 minutes, shaking/stirring often.

Note: use any summer vegetables or fresh herbs that you have on hand and if you like add chili flakes or hot sauce to the marinade.

potato vegetable casserole

In the summer I make this on the grill by wrapping the vegetables in foil paper. In the winter I tend to use the oven if I have it on to cook something else.

Serves 6

- **6 red skinned potatoes, washed and quartered**
- **1 large onion, peeled and thinly sliced**
- **2 stalks celery, chopped**
- **3 carrots, peeled and chopped**
- **1 red bell pepper, seeded and chopped**
- **1 cup sauerkraut**
- **1 teaspoon dried thyme**
- **1 tablespoon olive oil**
- **Salt & pepper to taste**
- **2 strips of bacon, cut in 1-inch pieces**

- Preheat oven to 375F.
- Place vegetables, herbs and oil in a casserole dish and season with salt and pepper. Stir to coat all vegetables with oil and seasoning. If you are using bacon, scatter the bacon on top of the vegetable mixture.
- Bake for 60 minutes.

garlic mashed potatoes

Garlic mashed potatoes are easy to make and tend to go well with so many main dishes.

Serves 4

> **6 yukon gold potatoes, peeled and chopped**
> **2 tablespoons butter**
> **3 cloves garlic, minced**
> **1-4 tablespoons milk (optional)**
> **Salt, to taste**
> **1 tablespoon chopped chives**

- In a large pot bring 6 cups of salted water to a boil. Add the potatoes and boil until tender (approximately 15 minutes).

- While the potatoes are cooking, melt butter in a small pan and sauté garlic over low heat for 1 minute. You do not want to brown the garlic, it is more about getting the garlic flavor through the butter.

- Drain potatoes and mash using a hand potato masher. Add the garlic butter and stir to mix well and remove any lumps. Stir in milk to get to desired consistency. Serve garnished with chives.

sweet potato fries

These "fries" are made with olive oil and baked instead of fried. So I like to think of them as a healthy.

Serves 4

>**3 large sweet potatoes, cut into wedges**
>>**(you can leave the skins on if you like)**
>
>**2 tablespoon olive oil**
>**2 cloves of garlic, finely chopped**
>**1 teaspoon ground cumin**
>**1 teaspoon dried thyme**
>**1 teaspoon cayenne pepper**
>**Salt, to taste**

- Preheat oven to 400F.

- Scatter potato wedges on a large baking sheet. Sprinkle with olive oil and stir to coat. Add remaining ingredients and stir to evenly season the fries. Spread the fries out so they are not overlapping.

- Bake for 30 minutes, shaking or stirring every 10 minutes.

potato au gratin

This is a great dish to serve with a baked ham. Also nice as a side with a grilled steak.

Serves 6
    1 teaspoon butter
    4 potatoes, peeled and sliced
    1 large onion, peeled and sliced
    3 tablespoon all purpose flour
    4 tablespoon Quaker Oats (Old Fashion)
    3 teaspoon dried sage
    Salt & pepper, to taste
    1 cup milk
    2 cups grated cheddar cheese

- Preheat oven to 350F.

- Grease a gratin dish with butter

- Place a layer of potato slices on bottom, sprinkle 1/3 of flour, oats and sage over potatoes. Season with salt and pepper then add a layer of onions.

- Repeat the previous step for two more layers. Pour milk over the top of potatoes and then cover with cheese.

- Bake for 90 minutes.

prosciutto wrapped asparagus

This is not only a nice side to serve with a grilled summer meal, but also makes a nice appetizer.

Serves 6
- **18 asparagus stalks**
- **1 teaspoon olive oil**
- **3 ounces prosciutto (thin slices)**
- **Salt, to taste**

- In a shallow pan, bring 2 cups of salted water to a boil. Add the asparagus and cook for 2 minutes. The asparagus should be bright green and very firm.

- Drain the asparagus and place in a boil of ice water to stop the cooking and capture that vibrant green color.

- When the asparagus have cooled, remove from water, pat dry and drizzle with olive oil. Wrap each stalk with prosciutto. Refrigerate until ready to serve.

soba noodles

These buckwheat noodles make a simple side dish to go with grilled meat.

Serves 4

- **1 package dried soba noodles**
- **2 teaspoons sesame oil**
- **1 tablespoon soy sauce**
- **3 green onions, chopped (green part only)**

- ✎ Boil soba noodles following instructions on package.

- ✎ Drain noodles and return to the pot. Over low heat toss noodles with oil and soy sauce. Add in chopped onion and toss for 1 more minute.

cilantro lime rice

Cilantro and lime really bring the rice to life. I like this with dishes like chicken mole or as a base for stuffed peppers.

Serves 6

> **2 cups white basmati rice**
> **4 cups water**
> **Zest of 2 limes**
> **1/4 teaspoon salt**
> **1/3 cup chopped fresh cilantro**
> **1 lime, cut in half and sliced**

- ❧ Bring water to boil. Add salt, lime zest and rice. Bring back to a boil then reduce heat to simmer, cover and simmer for 12 minutes or until all water is absorbed. Fluff rice with a fork and stir in cilantro, reserving a little for garnish.

- ❧ Serve garnished with a slice of lime and fresh cilantro.

Chapter 7 - Sides

mediterraean quinoa

I discovered quinoa a few years ago. Such a tasty, healthy grain that can be used in so many different recipes. Quinoa is gluten free and contains more protein than any other grain. In fact it is a complete protein with all nine essential amino acids.

Serves 4
>   **2 cups of water**
>   **½ teaspoon salt**
>   **1 cup of quinoa**
>   **½ cup sliced black olives**
>   **¼ cup chopped sun dried tomatoes packaged in olive oil (if purchased dry, soak in 2 tablespoons of olive oil for 30 minutes)**
>   **½ cup chopped marinated artichoke hearts**
>   **2 tablespoons artichoke marinade**

- Bring salted water to a boil and add quinoa. Stir and reduce heat to low. With lid on pot, gently boil for 15 minutes.

- Remove pot from heat, remove cover and add in remaining ingredients. Stir and replace the pot's cover letting the flavors blend for 15 minutes.

Note: This may be served with tossed green salad for a light lunch, or will lean grilled meat and side vegetable for a healthy supper.

spinach and gorgonzola risotto

by Pat & Pete Lareau, travel-and-eat.blogspot.com

*If you don't make risotto because of the constant stirring and slow addition of liquids,
try Pete's technique using a pressure cooker.*

Serves 6

2 tablespoons butter
1 tablespoon olive oil
3/4 cup chopped onion
1 cup Arborio rice
1/3 cup dry white wine
4 cups chicken stock
3/4 cup crumbled gorgonzola
3/4 cup chopped spinach leaves
1 1/2 tablespoons white balsamic vinegar

- Melt butter with oil in pressure cooker. Add onion and sauté until soft (3-4 minutes). Add rice and coat with butter and oil. Add stock and white wine and cover pressure cooker, turning heat to high.

- When pressure cooker reaches high pressure, cook for six minutes.

- Release pressure cooker top under running cold water (with top of pot tilted away from your face to avoid scalding when top is released).

- Stir and check consistency of rice, simmer a couple more minutes if too runny.

- Stir in crumbled gorgonzola, then stir in spinach and balsamic vinegar.

- Spoon risotto into bowls and garnish with a few shavings of gorgonzola or parmesan (and parsley, if desired).

smoked salmon risotto

I decided to test out Pete's risotto recipe to create a smoked salmon dish. It was the easiest risotto I ever made and it gave me a reason to use a pressure cooker. This could be served as a complete lunch dish.

Serves 6

     2 tablespoons butter
     1 tablespoon olive oil
     3/4 cup chopped onion
     1 cup Arborio rice
     1/3 cup dry white wine
     4 cups chicken stock
     1 cup chopped smoked salmon
     3/4 cup crumbled goat cheese
     1/4 cup chopped chives

- Melt butter with oil in pressure cooker. Add onion and sauté until soft (3-4 minutes). Add rice and coat with butter and oil. Add stock and white wine and cover pressure cooker, turning heat to high.

- When pressure cooker reaches high pressure, cook for six minutes.

- Release pressure cooker top under running cold water (with top of pot tilted away from your face to avoid scalding when top is released).

- Stir and check consistency of rice, simmer a couple more minutes if too runny.

- Stir in salmon, cheese and chives. Spoon risotto into bowls and serve.

Note: You can follow Pete's basic recipe/technique and add ingredients at the end to create a wide range of risotto recipes. Wild mushroom with cream is the next one I'll try.

pad thai

You make this recipe as an entrée if you add additional shrimp and perhaps a little chicken and/or pork. This is a recipe that can be prepared mild or spicy, adjust to your taste.

Serves 6

1 package rice noodles
1 tablespoons oil
2 cloves garlic, peeled and minced
1/2 pound shrimp, peeled
1 egg
1 carrot, peeled and grated
1/2 cup chopped fresh basil
1/2 cup chopped peanuts
1 green onion, chopped
1/4 cup bean sprouts

Sauce

1/2 cup hot water
1 tablespoon tamarind paste
3 tablespoons fish sauce
2 tablespoons Sriracha hot sauce
3 tablespoons brown sugar

- Soak rice noodles in water for 10 minutes.
- Make the sauce while the noodles soften. Pour the hot water into a small mixing bowl or glass measuring cup. Add the tamarind paste and stir well to dissolve. Add the other sauce ingredients and stir to dissolve. (Note that you will need all the sugar to balance out the intense sourness of the tamarind.)
- Heat the oil in a large wok. Add the garlic and sauté for one minute. Add the shrimp and sauté until they just begin to turn pink. Remove shrimp from the pan and scramble the egg in the hot pan. Remove the egg and add the sauce to the wok. Add the noodles and stir to coat with sauce. Stir for 5 minutes then add the shrimp and eggs. Stir for 1 more minute.
- Serve on a platter topped with the remaining ingredients.

Chapter 7 - Sides

lima beans with fennel

Lima beans are something I didn't enjoy as a child. I think it may have been that no one had this recipe. This pairs extremely well with grilled lamb chops or elk steaks.

Serves 6

1/3 cup olive oil
1 small onion, chopped
1 fresh fennel bulb, trimmed and sliced
3 cups frozen baby lima beans, thawed
1 teaspoon ground fennel seeds
1 cup chicken stock
1/2 cup white wine
2 tablespoons fresh chopped dill
1/4 cup chopped sundried tomatoes
1/2 teaspoon dried sage
2 tablespoons lemon juice
Salt & pepper, to taste

- Heat oil in a large pan over medium heat. Add onion and fennel bulb and sauté for 5 minutes. Add lima beans, fennel seeds and sauté 3 minutes. Add stock, wine and dill. Bring to a boil and then reduce heat to simmer for 10 minutes.

- Stir in tomatoes and sage and simmer for 15 minutes longer.

- Just prior to serving stir in lemon juice and add salt and pepper.

Desserts

Paso Robles offers beautiful sunsets to enjoy each evening. After the sunsets, the country skies light up with stars, making it the perfect time to sip wine and perhaps enjoy a little something sweet to end the evening.

mascarpone with dark honey and blueberries - 164
liquid love blackberry snow - 165
baked apples filled with dried fruit and nuts - 166
baked pears with blue cheese - 167
grilled figs - 168
berry turnovers - 169
crème brûlée -171
rustic nut tart - 173
nancy's apple torte - 174
brulée de figue - 175
apple cake with caramel sauce - 176
fresh peach cobbler - 177
baklava -179
chocolate cheesecake - 181
frannie's chocolate almond torte - 183
sozinho chocolate cake - 185
dark chocolate pie - 187

mascarpone with dark honey and blueberries
by Pete & Pat Lareau, travel-and-eat.blogspot.com

I didn't think I even liked mascarpone until Pat make this dessert for me!

A good quality, dark honey really makes this recipe. Fresh blueberries with the honey and mascarpone make a simple yet tasty dessert.

Makes 6 Servings

3/4 pound mascarpone cheese, room temperature
3 cups fresh blueberries
1/2 cup dark honey (lavender or wildflower)

- Pipe mascarpone cheese decoratively into bowls or glass sherbet cups.

- Drizzle with dark wildflower honey.

- Top each with a small handful of blueberries.

eat this with...

Le Vigne Sparkling
Pomar Junction Late Harvest Viognier

liquid love blackberry snow
by Chef Marc LeDuc, Tobin James Cellars

A surprise treat to wow your Summer BBQ guests.
When Liquid Love comes out, anything can happen!

Serves 12

> **6 pints blackberries**
> **1/2 cup raw honey**
> **1 cup Liquid Love Late Harvest Zinfandel**

- Place a 9 x 12 dish in the freezer to chill.

- In a small sauce pan, simmer the berries and the Liquid Love until the berries are all broken down and the alcohol has evaporated.

- Strain out the seeds through a fine sieve.

- Place in chilled pan and place back in freezer until frozen solid.

- Using the edge of an ice cream scoop scrape the frozen berries making a snow.

- Serve with a glass of liquid love to make a perfect pairing.

eat this with...

Tobin James Liquid Love
Late Harvest Zinfandel

baked apples filled with dried fruit and nuts

The caramel-wine sauce really makes this recipe special; however, if you want to reduce the sweetness simply use unsweetened apple juice with a little honey instead.

eat this with...
Calacreous Chardonnay
Pretty-Smith Tawny-style Port
Tablas Creek Vin de Paille

Makes 4 servings

1/2 cup butter
1/4 cup dark brown sugar
1 cup white wine
4 large Golden Delicious apples
2 tablespoons walnut pieces
1 tablespoon dried apricots, chopped
1 tablespoon dried figs, chopped
Vanilla ice cream (optional)

- Preheat oven to 350F.

- Melt butter in a small sauce pan and stir in sugar. Continue to stir and bring to a boil then gradually stir in wine. Bring back to a boil, continually stirring. Remove from heat.

- Wash and core the apples but do not peel. place the apples in a 9-inch round glass pie dish.

- Mix the dried fruit and nuts and fill the apple centers, sprinkling any remaining mixture over the top of apples.

- Pour the sauce into the pan. Be sure to coat each apple top.

- Bake for approximately 1 hour, occasionally basting with sauce.

- Serve with warm sauce from pan spooned on top.

baked pears with blue cheese

Pears baked with blue cheese, nuts, honey and wine make a delightful dessert. I've also made this recipe as a salad course, unbaked and without the sauce, simply with a drizzle of honey. When my neighbor's tree is loaded with pears I tend to make a lot of pear dishes. Her pears are the best but all seem to ripen at once.

Serves 4

4 Bartlett pears
3 tablespoons blue cheese crumbles
4 tablespoons pecan pieces
3 tablespoons honey
2 cups of white wine
4 tablespoons pear butter (optional)

- Preheat oven to 350F.

- In a small sauce pan warm the wine and stir in honey.

- Mix cheese crumbles with nuts.

- Wash pears and cut bottoms off so they will sit flat in the pan. Cut the top off approximately 1 inch down, save the tops for later. Scoop out the core and create enough space to stuff each pear with almost 2 tablespoons of nut mixture. Place pears in 9-inch diameter glass pie pan.

- Stuff each pear with nut mixture and place top bake on. Pour honey wine sauce over top and bake for approximately 30 minutes. Baste with wine sauce every 10 minutes. The pears should be warm all the way through but still maintain their shape.

- Serve on a plate smeared with pear butter.

eat this with...
AronHill Vinho Doce
Graveyard Deliverance
Pear Valley Belle Fin

grilled figs

When figs are in season, this is a dessert that takes only a couple of minutes to make and is a nice little bite to have after a large dinner.

Serves 4

6 figs
6 teaspoons fresh goat cheese
3 teaspoons honey

- Wash figs and cut in half lengthwise and drizzle with honey.

- Place figs on baking sheet and place under broil until they jsut begin to turn golden on top.

- Top each fig half with goat cheese and return to the broiler until cheese begins to soften and have a slightly toasted appearance. it doesn't take long, so watch carefully!

- Serve on a plate drizzled with a little honey. A fun little dessert you can eat with your fingers.

eat this with...
Bodegas Paso Robles Trousseau
Cass Late Harvest Roussanne
Pear Valley Frizzante Muscat
Pretty-Smith Port (tawny-style)
Rotta Black Monukka

berry turnovers

It is hard to go wrong with hot gooey berries inside a light flaky crust!

Serves 6

1 package of frozen puff pastry
3 cups frozen mixed berries
1 cup Port or fruity wine
1/4 cup maple syrup
Whipped cream

Note: I like the mix of tart and sweet. If you prefer a sweeter dessert just add sugar to the berry wine mixture.

- Place frozen berries in a bowl and pour wine over top. Let the berries thaw and absorb the wine for approximately 2 hours.

- Thaw pastry sheets on counter for 40 minutes

- While pastry is thawing, place the berries along with the juice, in a small sauce pan, bring to a boil then reduce to simmer. Simmer until juice reduces by half (approximately 30 minutes).

- Preheat oven to 400F.

- Lightly flour counter top or work surface. Spread pastry sheets on floured surface and cut each sheet in three pieces along the fold line and then in half. You should have 12 rectangles. Bake puff pastry until it puffs and turns golden (approximately 15 minutes).

- When pastry is cool enough to handle, place one rectangle on each plate, cover with berries, drizzle with syrup, top with cream, place another rectangle on top, drizzle more maple syrup and top with whipped cream.

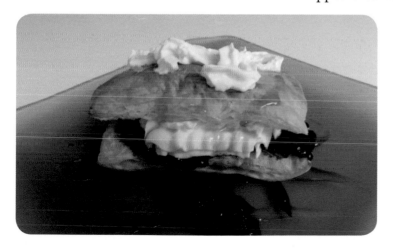

eat this with...
AronHill Vinho Doce
Calcareous Cabernet Sauvignon
Tobin James Liquid Love

crème brûlée

There are so many different combinations of eggs, cream and sugar to make a Crème Brûlée. Over the years I've tweaked my recipe to find the perfect texture. While many recipes will use at least a portion of half and half, I really believe whipping cream all on its own works best. Although vanilla is the most common flavor, try something different like orange zest or chocolate to wow your guests. The really fun part is using a torch in the kitchen.

Makes 8 servings
Base ingredients
3 cups whipping cream
3/4 cup fine sugar
6 large egg yolks
For the Brûlée
8 teaspoons golden raw sugar
Topping ideas (optional)
Fresh berries
Berries soaked in dessert wine

Flavor Ingredients
Vanilla Crème Brûlée
1 vanilla bean split lengthwise
Orange Zest Crème Brûlée
Zest of one lemon
2 teaspoons vanilla extract
Chocolate Crème Brûlée
8 ounces semisweet chocolate, finely chopped
2 teaspoons vanilla extract

- Preheat oven to 325F.
- Arrange eight 3/4-cup ramekins in a 12x9x2-inch baking pan.
- Place cream in a small saucepan with a heavy bottom. Add your desired flavor ingrients, and over low heat, bring to simmer.
- Whisk sugar and yolks in a large bowl until thick (about 3 minutes). **Gradually** whisk in the hot cream mixture. Let stand for 10 minutes.
- Pour mixture through strainer, then divide among ramekins.
- Pour enough hot water into the pan to come halfway up the sides of the ramekins to ensure even baking.
- Bake until just set (about 50 minutes). Remove from pan and chill, uncovered for 2 hours. Cover and refrigerate for an additional 2 hours or overnight.
- Sprinkle raw sugar on top and torch. Refrigerate for an additional 1-2 hours.

eat this with...

Cass Late Harvest Roussanne
Eberle Muscat Canelli
Pear Valley Orange Muscat
Ranchita Canyon Cabernet Sauvignon Port
Robert Hall Orange Muscat
Vina Robles Petite Sirah

rustic nut tart by Maggie D'Ambrosia, Windward Vineyard

The rustic appearnce of this nut tart creation by Maggie adds to the elegance and charm.

Crust
1 ½ cups flour
8 + 2 tablespoons unsalted butter
¼ cup ice water

Filling
3 cups toasted, chopped nuts (pecan, walnut)
1 cup light brown sugar, packed
¼ cup chopped orange peel
1 teaspoon lemon zest
¼ cup honey
3 eggs

eat this with...

Windward Vineyard Estate Pinot Noir

- For the crust: Blend flour & salt. Cut in 8 tablespoons butter using 2 knives scissor-fashion until mixture resembles coarse meal. Then add remaining butter & cut in until size of large peas. Add ice water, 1 tablespoon at a time until moist clumps form. Gather into ball; flatten into disk. Wrap in plastic; let stand 1 hour (do not chill).

- For the filling: Mix first 4 ingredients in medium bowl. Whisk eggs & honey in another medium bowl. Add egg mixture to nut mixture; stir until well blended.

- Position rack in center of oven and preheat to 375F. Roll crust out on lightly floured surface to 14-inch round. Transfer to 11-inch diameter tart pan with removable bottom, allowing crust to drape over pan. Pour filling into crust, spreading evenly. Pull edges over filling and drape randomly.

- Bake on middle rack for 40 minutes or until light golden brown (cover the edges with foil as necessary if crust becomes too brown).

nancy's apple torte by Neils & Bimmer Udsen, Castoro Cellars

Nancy Dwyer, a good friend of the Udsens has been making this for years and it has become a "staple" in their households every Fall. The torte is fairly easy to make and has a very impressive presentation.

Crust
- **1 cup flour**
- **¼ cup sugar**
- **½ teaspoon vanilla**
- **1 stick butter (8 tablespoons)**

Filling
- **1 egg**
- **¼ cup sugar**
- **1 teaspoon vanilla**
- **8 oz cream cheese**

Topping
- **3 Granny Smith apples**
- **2 tablespoons sugar**
- **1 tablespoon cinnamon**

- ❧ Pre-heat oven to 425F
- ❧ In a food processer mix all crust ingredients. Press dough in bottom of 9 inch spring form pan.
- ❧ In food processor mix all filling ingredients. Pour onto crust.
- ❧ Peel, core and slice 3 Granny Smith apples for topping. Coat with sugar and cinnamon. Arrange sliced apples in a circle.
- ❧ Bake at 425F for 10 minutes. Reduce temperature of oven to 375F and bake for an additional 25 minutes. Serve cold.

eat this with...
Castoro Cellars
Late Harvest Muscat Canelli

brulée de figue

by Chef Jacob, Cass Winery

Caramelized fig with almond praline & fresh goat cheese. Another simple dish from Chef Jacob that looks neat on a plate, tastes delicious, and is relatively easy to prepare.

Serves 4

6 fresh black mission figs
2 tablespoons sugar
4 tablespoons chevre
½ cup almond pralines
A berry coulis garnish might brighten this plate, if desired.

- Cut the figs in half and place them on a baking sheet, cut side up. Sprinkle them with a generous amount of sugar.

- Using a brulee torch, gently torch each fig top until the sugars begin to liquify and carmelize. Let them cool for a few minutes before touching.

- Place 3 fig halves in the center of each plate, in a triangle shape. Smear a dollup of fresh chevre onto each fig. Crumble the pralines over the entire dish.

eat this with...
Cass Late Harvest Roussanne

apple cake with caramel sauce
by Beverly Steinbeck, Steinbeck Vineyards & Winery

The Steinbeck family's six-generation agricultural roots run deep in Paso Robles. Three generations farm the large vineyard acreage and produce a small amount of premium wines annually. Try this sweet, warm cake recipe by Beverly for your family.

eat this with...
Steinbeck Viognier

Cake	Sauce
2 cups flour	**1 tablespoon flour**
2 cups sugar	**½ cup brown sugar**
1 teaspoon baking soda	**½ cup granulated sugar**
1 teaspon salt	**½ cup cream**
½ cup vegetable oil	**½ cup butter**
2 teaspoons cinnamon	
2 eggs	
4 cups peeled, thinly sliced apples	

- Preheat oven to 350F

- Stir all of the cake ingredients together in a medium sized mixing bowl, reserving the apples for later. The mixture will be very thick. Add the apples and stir to evenly combine.

- Pour the cake mixture into a 9 X 13 greased pyrex pan and bake for 50 minutes.

- Combine all sauce ingredients in a small sauce pan. Bring to a boil for 2 minutes, continuously stirring.

- Serve cake warm with warm caramel sauce and whipped cream.

Note: The Steinbeck family offers tours of their historic property in addition to wine tasting in a large room filled with family treasures.

fresh peach cobbler by Mitchella Vineyard & Winery

Cobbler has never tasted so good. When fresh peaches are in season, this recipe served with ice cream and Mitchella's White Port is the perfect way to end the day.

Serves 6-8

½ cup unsalted butter
1 cup all-purpose flour
2 cups sugar
3 teaspoons baking powder
½ teaspoon salt
1 cup milk

5 cups fresh peeled and thinly sliced peaches
2 tablespoons lemon juice
4 cardamom seeds
½ teaspoon vanilla
1 teaspoon cinnamon
½ teaspoon fresh ground nutmeg
1 pint French vanilla ice cream
1 375ml Riportella Bianco or other White Port

- Preheat Oven to 375F

- Melt the butter in a 13x9x2 baking dish. Combine the flour, 1 cup sugar, baking powder, and salt, mix thoroughly. Add the milk and mix with a fork until just combined. Pour over the melted butter, do not mix.

- In a sauce pan add 1 cup sugar, the peaches, lemon juice, cardamom seeds, and vanilla, bring to a boil and simmer for 5 minutes. Remove the cardamom seeds and pour the peaches evenly over the butter and flour mixture, do not mix. Sprinkle with the cinnamon and nutmeg, bake for 45-50 minutes until golden brown.

- Spoon two large spoonfuls of cobbler onto a plate or bowl, top with one scoop of French Vanilla Ice Cream, then splash 1 ounce of Riportella Bianco over the top. Enjoy!

eat this with...
Mitchella Riportella Bianco

baklava

Don't let working with phyllo dough stop you from making this decidant traditional Greek dessert. This is one of those desserts that gets better with time, so be sure to make it at least one day ahead.

Syrup

- 1 cup honey
- 1/2 cup water
- 1/2 cup sugar
- 1/2 teaspoon groudn cinnamon
- 1 tablespoon lemon juice
- Peel of one lemon (without pith)
- Peel of one orange (without pith)

Filling

- 2 cups coarsley ground walnuts
- 1 cup coarsley ground almonds
- 1 cup coarsley ground peacans
- 2 tablespoons sugar
- 1/2 teaspoon ground cinnamon
- 1/2 teaspoon ground cloves
- 2 tablespoons melted butter

Pastry

- 1 package phyllo dough, thawed
- 3/4 pound unsalted butter, melted
- 1/2 teaspoon ground cloves
- 30 pine nuts

eat this with...

Pretty-Smith Zinfandel Port (Tawny style)
Mitchella Riportella Bianco
Tablas Creek Vin de Paille

- Make the syrup first so it can come to room temperature. In a small sauce pan, combine the honey, sugar and water. Bring to a boil, stirring occasionally. Add the lemon juice, cinnamon and peel. Reduce heat and simmer for 20 minutes. It should have a syrup consistency. Remove peel and let cool.
- Mix nuts, sugar, cinnamon, nutmeg, cloves and butter together in a glass bowl.
- Place phyllo on counter and cover with a damp towel to keep it moist while you create the baklava.
- Preheat oven to 325F.
- Brush a 14x9 inch baking pan with melted butter.
- Place 8 phyllo sheets on the bottom of the pan, brushing each sheet generously with butter. Take an additional 4 sheets and place in pan allowing sheets to drape over each side of the pan. Brush with melted butter. Pour half of the filling into the pan and spread evenly. Fold the sheets draping over the sides on top of the filling. Brush with butter.
- Repeat the previous instruction, beginning with 8 phyllo sheets to create another layer with filling. Top with an additional 8 sheets, brushing each with butter. Tuck the sheets around the sides.
- Score through the top layers of pastry to make diamond shaped pieces. Sprinkle ground cloves and place a pine nut on each piece.
- Bake for 1 hour then allow to cool for 5 minutes before pouring syrup over pastry. Allow to stand overnight then cut through scored pieces.

chocolate cheesecake

I've been making cheesecake for as long as I can remember. I made this, when I was in high school, as a birthday present for my very first boyfriend and the men in my life have been fighting for leftovers ever since. Be sure to plan ahead since the cheesecake needs to age at least 2 days to gain flavor.

Crust

1 package chocolate wafers (3 cups)
1/2 cup butter, melted

Filling

2 ounces bittersweet chocolate
1/4 cup strong hot espresso
5 eggs
1/4 cup sugar
1 pound cream cheese
2/3 cup sugar
1 tablespoon lemon juice
1/4 cup all purpose flour
1 teaspoon vanilla extract
1 cup sour cream

Topping

Fresh berries, whipped cream, chocolate sauce....your choice!

- Preheat oven to 325F.
- Use food processor to turn wafers into crumbs then mix in melted butter. Press into bottom and sides of 9 inch round pan with removable ring.
- Melt chocolate in hot espresso (on stove top or in microwave), stir and set aside
- Separate egg whites and yolks (you will use them all).
- Using a mixer, beat egg whites and sugar until stiff. Add the cream cheese and mix until well blended, then beat in egg yolks one at a time. Gradually beat in the remaining ingredients including the chocolate in espresso.
- Pour filling into pan with crust. Bake until set (1 to 1.5 hours).
- Cool on countertop then remove the ring, place in an air tight container and age in refrigerator for at least 2 days.

Note: This recipe can be easily converted to a traditional cheesecake by making the following changes:

- *Use graham crackers instead of chocolate wafers*
- *Omit the chocolate and espresso*
- *Increase lemon juice to 3 tablespoons*
- *Increase vanilla to 3 teaspoons*

eat this with...

Pear Valley Frizzante Muscat
Paso Port Zinfandel
Roxo Ruby Tradicional
Vina Robles Petite Sirah

frannie's chocolate almond torte

by Dana Brown, Calcareous Vineyard

Dana and Frannie started with an old family recipe for an almond torte . After experimenting with the recipe and chocolate, they came up with this new recipe to complement their Cabernet Sauvignon.

3 ounces bittersweet chocolate
2 ½ teaspoons instant espresso powder
1 tablespoon +1 teaspoon water
½ cup butter
7 ounces almond paste
¾ cup extra fine baker's sugar
3 eggs
¼ cup flour
½ teaspoon baking powder

Icing

1 ounce bittersweet chocolate
1 teaspoon espresso powder
1 teaspoon water
¼ cup butter
1 tablespoon unsweetened cocoa powder
2 tablespoon heavy whipping cream
1 cup powdered sugar

¼ cup almonds

- Pre-heat oven to 350F.

- Dissolve espresso powder in water in a double boiler. Add chocolate and butter then heat, stirring continually, until melted and smooth.

- In a separate bowl mix almond paste with sugar until smooth, add the eggs and mix. Add chocolate mixture and stir well. Sift flour and baking powder into mixture and stir. Do not over beat.

- Butter and flour a round 8" baking pan. Pour mixture in and bake at 350F for 40-45 minutes. Let cool 5 minutes. Run a knife around the sides and turn onto a plate. Cool before icing.

- For Icing: Dissolve espresso powder in water. Add chocolate and butter, melt in a double boiler until smooth. Add cocoa powder, stir until combined. Add whipping cream and beat the mixture for 2 minutes. Add powdered sugar and beat until smooth. Frost cake. Toast almonds in the oven until golden. Let almonds cool. Grind almonds to a fine powder. Sprinkle on top of the icing.

eat this with...
Calcareous Cabernet Sauvignon

sozinho chocolate cake by Steve Kroener, Silver Horse

This decandent chocolate cake made with the very Port it is served with can only be described as yummy! Who knew Steve was a baker?

12 servings

- 2/3 cup boiling water
- 3 ounces unsweetened chocolate
- 8 tablespoons (1 stick) sweet butter
- 1 teaspoon vanilla extract
- 2 cups granulated sugar
- 2 eggs, separated

- 1 teaspoon baking soda
- 1/2 cup sour cream
- 1/3 cup Silver Horse Winery's Sozinho Port
- 2 cups less 2 tablespoons unbleached, all-purpose flour, sifted
- 1 teaspoon baking powder
- Chocolate frosting of your choice

- Preheat oven to 350 degrees.

- Grease and flour the sides of a 10 inch cake pan with removeable ring. Place round sheet of parchment on the bottom of the pan.

- Pour boiling water over the chocolate and butter in a medium sized bowl. Let stand until melted. Stir in vanilla and sugar, then whisk in egg yolks, one at a time, blending well after each addition.

- Mix baking soda, sour cream, and Sozinho Port in a small bowl then whisk into chocolate mixture.

- Sift flour and baking powder together and add to batter, mixing thoroughly.

eat this with...
Silver Horse Winery Sozinho Port

- Beat egg whites until stiff but not dry. Stir a quarter of the egg whites thoroughly into batter. Scoop the remaining egg whites on top of the batter and gently fold together.

- Pour batter into prepared pan. Set on the middle rack of the oven and bake for 40 to 50 minutes, or until the edges have pulled away from the sides of the pan and a cake tester inserted into the center comes out clean.

- Cool in pan for 10 minutes, unmold, remove parchment paper and cool completely before frosting.

dark chocolate pie by Pat & Pete Lareau, travel-and-eat.blogspot.com

This extremely rich dessert is for the chocolate lovers. Each time Pat revises the recipe I swear it gets richer. Be sure to serve small pieces and you can always freeze any leftovers.

12 servings

- 3/4 cup heavy cream
- 1 1/2 cups milk
- 6 large egg yolks
- 2/3 cup packed light brown sugar
- 1 teaspoon vanilla extract
- 1 tablespoon instant espresso powder
- 4 teaspoon cornstarch
- 4 tablespoon unsweetened cocoa powder
- 6 ounces bittersweet chocolate, chopped
- 3 tablespoons unsalted butter

Chocolate Crust

- Non-stick spray
- 6 tablespoons (3/4 stick) unsalted butter
- 1 ounce bittersweet chocolate, chopped
- 30 chocolate wafer cookies

- Spray 9-inch-diameter glass pie dish with nonstick spray. Stir butter and chocolate in heavy small saucepan over low heat until melted. Finely grind cookies in processor. Add chocolate mixture. Process until crumbs are moistened. Press crumb mixture into prepared pie dish. Freeze until firm, about 30 minutes.

- Heat all of the cream and 1-1/4 cups of the milk to boiling and remove from heat.

- Whisk egg yolks, brown sugar, vanilla, and remaining 1/4 cup of milk in another sauce pan. Whisk in the cocoa powder, espresso powder and cornstarch until blended. Gradually whisk in hot milk.

- Return to heat and whisk constantly until mixture thickens and boils. Remove from heat. Add chocolate and butter. Whisk until melted and smooth.

- Pour filling into frozen chocolate crust. Refrigerate at least 4 hours. Can be made and kept chilled and covered for one day.

- Serve topped with whipped cream, berries, nuts and/or praline nibs.

eat this with...

AronHill Vinho Doce
Pear Valley Orange Muscat
Ranchita Canyon Cabernet Sauvignon Port
San Marcos Creek Late Harvest Zin
Silver Horse Sozinho Port
Tobin James Liquid Love

Winery Menus

The wineries of Paso Robles frequently showcase their wines by serving them with food. In this chapter you will find menus with wine paired by twenty different Paso Robles wineries. Pick a menu, invite your favorite friends and try these wine inspired menus.

ARONHILL
Vineyards

Tuscan Cuisine

This Itailian inspired menu will have your guests saying "delizioso".

Arugula & Shaved Parmesan Salad
dressed with a Tuscan Vinaigrette p75
AronHill Melange de Blanc

Portabella Mushroom, Onion
and Red Pepper on a warm Ciabatta Roll p36
AronHill Cabernet Sauvignon

Fettuccini di Mare p109
AronHill Primitivo

Chocolate Gelato topped with
Port soaked Berries
AronHill Vinho Doce

AronHill Vineyards

The Power of Intention;
The Fruits of Patience;
The Taste of Passion.

At AronHill winemaking begins with Intention, Patience and Passion. The team strives to create bold, luscious varietals and blends from the estate vineyards to proudly present as the jewels of AronHill.

The tasting room offers panaramic views of the vineyards and surrounding hills from both the spacious, inside tasting bar and the outside patio with bistro tables. Enjoy cheese plates and other light fare as you feel all the positive energy.

Visit soon to enliven your heart, awaken your palate, tantalize your taste buds and stir your passions.

Open Daily 11am - 5pm
3745 West Highway 46, Templeton
aronhillvineyards.com   805.434.3066

BODEGAS
PASO ROBLES

Spanish Small Plates

This small plates dinner menu paired with Bodegas Paso Robles wines puts a Californian twist on Spanish classics.

Grilled Shrimp with Garlic Wine Sauce p49
Bodegas Paso Robles Galicia - Albariño

Mussels with Chorizo p46
*Bodegas Robles ¡Viva Yo! - a blend of Tempranillo
and Cabernet Sauvignon*

Rosemary Lamb Chops p128
served with Fennel Lima Beans
*Bodegas Paso Robles Iberia - a blend of Touriga Nacional,
Tempranillo, Graciano and Tinto Cão*

Cheese Plate: Figs topped with Goat Cheese,
Manchego with Quince, Picón and Spanish Almonds
Bodegas Paso Robles Trousseau - Bastardo

"People always ask: why Tempranillo? Where's the Cabernet?" Dorothy Schuler, owner and winemaker at Bodegas Paso Robles, always has the same answer. *"California was settled by the Spanish because it looks like home to them. The same rolling golden hills, the same climate, the absolutely perfect location to grow Tempranillo and all the other Spanish native grapes. All we're missing are the black bulls!"*

Dorothy takes the classic Spanish grapes and adds a New World twist, producing wines that are made specifically to pair with food, but California in style. She believes that more and more Americans are embracing the Old World concept that *"wine is a food."* And that wine is the quintessential part of the meal that makes a great dinner memorable. Bon apetito!

Sunday - Thursday 12 - 6pm
Friday - Sunday 12 - 8pm
729 13th Street, Paso Robles
805.237.3790   bodegaspasorobles.com

CALCAREOUS
VINEYARD

Winemaker's Dinner

Invite your favorite friends to enjoy this delightful menu paired with Calcareous wines.

Spicy Crab Cakes with
Basil Orange Ailoli p43
Calcareous Viognier/Marsanne

Roasted Tomato and Pepper Soup p90
Calcareous Syrah

Fennel Shortribs served with p134
Oven Roasted Potatoes and Onions
*Calcareous Meritage - a blend of Cabernet Sauvignon, Merlot,
Cabernet Franc, Malbec and Petit Verdot*

Frannie's Chocolate Almond Torte p183
Calcareous Cabernet Sauvignon

Calcareous Vineyard is named as a tribute to the estate's terroir. The 442 acre estate begins three miles west of Paso Robles and stretches several miles west towards the Pacific Ocean. The limestone soil and the varied microclimates allow Calcareous to produce Bordeaux, Rhone and Burgundy varietal simultaneously.

The family winery has an uncompromising commitment to quality and wines of authentic vineyard expression.

Visit the tasting room to enjoy panoramic views and experience the award winning wines.

Tasting Room Open
Daily 11am - 5pm

3430 Peachy Canyon Road
Paso Robles, CA
805.239.0289
calcareous.com

CASS
Vineyard & Winery

CASS
Vineyard & Winery

Cuisine du Rhône

*Chef Jacob takes you to the south of France with this exquisite
wine paired dinner featuring traditional Rhône dishes.*

L'un - *La Soupe Froide de de Pois p89*
Cold pea soup, crispy shallots and blue crab claws
Cass Rockin One Blanc - a blend of Roussanne and Marsanne

Deux - *La Salade Lyonnais p70*
House-cured bacon, soft poached egg on
a frisée bed with dijon vinaigrette
Cass Rockin One - a blend of Mourvèdre, Grenache, and Syrah

Intervalle - *Glace Aux Pêches Fraiche*
Fresh peach and mint Ice
Cass Roussanne

Quatre - *Grillards de Bœuf p140*
Adelaida Hills, grass-fed beef. Topped with seared Foie Gras,
wine soaked mushrooms, sautéed chard,
pommes dauphinoises
*Cass Edge - a blend of Cabernet Sauvignon,
Cabernet Franc, Merlot, Petit Verdot and Malbec*

Doux - *Brulée de Figue p175*
Caramelized fig with hazlenut praline & fresh goat cheese
Cass Late Harvest Roussanne

Cass Vineyards and Winery is located in the rolling, oak-studded hills between Paso Robles and Creston. This area that the vineyard calls home offers quiet serenity for the visitor and a perfect growing season for wine grapes. The winery specializes in estate-grown Rhône varietals and blends.

Offering a unique tasting exerience, visitors to the tasting room may also enjoy the Cass Café. The café is open for lunches every day from 12pm to 4pm or by reservation. Chef Jacob Lovejoy is creating a variety of specialty plates from crab cakes to smoked chicken salad, there is something for everyone. Each menu item is specially paired with a glass of Cass Wine. The café is also able to host private parties and events.

Tasting Room Open
Mon-Fri 12 pm - 5 pm
Sat-Sun 11 am - 6 pm

7350 Linne Rd, Paso Robles,
805.239.1730   casswines.com

CASTORO CELLARS

DAM FINE WINE

Italy Meets Brazil

by Niels & Bimmer Udsen

"Our families are spread around the world. During a family gathering in Tuscany we enjoyed this flank steak but in our version we added a Brazilian twist! While visiting Niels' brother in Brazil (30 year resident) we noticed the lime marinade and loved it."

Bufala Mozzarella and Heirloom Tomatoes *p79*
Castoro Cellars Pinot Grigio

Butter Lettuce Salad *p68*
Castoro Cellars Viognier

Grilled Flank Steak with Shaved Parmesan Cheese *p143*
and Arugula served with Fresh Herb Roasted Potatoes
and Savory Oven Roasted Zucchini
Castoro Cellars Primitivo

Nancy's Apple Torte *p174*
Castoro Cellars Late Harvest Muscat Canelli

Castoro Cellars' Mediterranean style Tasting Room is located in the heart of the Paso Robles Wine Country. Follow the path under the 100 foot long grape arbor into the cozy tasting room where the resident cat can be found lounging in front of the large stone fireplace. There is always a varied selection of new releases, single vineyard and library wines to be enjoyed. Being proud stewards of the environment, their tasting room is powered by solar panels and the grapes are sourced from both organic and sustainably grown grapes.

You'll find local artisan products, interesting gifts and gourmet food items. A spacious art gallery featuring local artists can be found next to the tasting room, and outside the large gardens offer ample space to picnic while relishing the sprawling country views.

Open Daily 10am - 5:30pm
1315 N. Bethel Road,
Templeton (off HWY 46 West)
888-DAM-FINE
castorocellars.com

EBERLE WINERY

Winemaker's Dinner

Gary and Marcy Eberle love to entertain guests with food and wine. This menu is sure to please your friends.

White bean and tuna stuffed tomatoes p39
served on a bed of greens
*Eberle Côtes-du-Rôbles Blanc - a blend of
Grenache Blanc and Viognier*

Smoked Scallops wrapped in Prociutto p47
Eberle Viognier

Gary's Paella p115
Eberle Cabernet Sauvignon

Orange Zest Crème Brûlée p171
Eberle Muscat Canelli

A pioneer of the Paso Robles California wine appellation, Gary Eberle has been making premium Paso Robles wines for more than 35 years. Today, Eberle is one of the highest award-winning wineries in the U.S.A. and Gary Eberle is credited as the first U.S. winemaker to produce a 100% Syrah.

Nestled on 60 rolling acres on Highway 46 East, Eberle Winery remains one of the longest privately owned wineries in Paso Robles with an annual production of 25,000 cases. Most wines produced are 100% varietal and aged in 17,000 square feet of underground caves; offering proof that Gary's motto is, "the wine in the bottle should taste like the grape on the vine." Visit Eberle Winery and you'll likely share a toast with Gary, his wife Marcy, and their two Standard Poodles. Eberle Winery is open for weddings and private events and offers complimentary wine tasting and cave tours.

Open Daily
Winter 10am-5pm ~ Summer 10am-6pm
3810 Highway 46 East, Paso Robles
805.238.9607   eberlewinery.com

Late Summer Dinner
Graveyard Vineyards

Set a table on the porch and enjoy this late summer menu with family and friends.

A Light Beginning
Sauteed Scallops with orange sauce
served on a bed of greens p74
Graveyard Paso Tombstone White, an aromatic white blend of Sauvignon Blanc, Gewurztraminer and Muscat

Spicy Second
Chorizo Stuffed Peppers
with cilanto rice and manchego cheese p55
Graveyard Paso Tombstone Red, a blend of Cabernet Sauvignon and Syrah with a touch of Petite Sirah

Hearty Entrée
Braised short ribs served
with garlic smashed potatoes
and roasted carrots p135
Graveyard Dark Phantom, "monster" Petite Sirah

A Sweet Ending
Baked pears with blue cheese,
nuts & honey p167
Graveyard Deliverance, chocolate infused Port

Graveyard Vineyards is a small family winery owned by Rob and Paula Campbell-Taylor. Located above the historic Pleasant Valley Cemetery, just 6 minutes from Highway 46 East and Airport Road, the winery is so warm and welcoming you will feel like you are visiting an old friend on your very first visit.

The award winning wines like the Sauvignon Blanc, Paso Tombstone White, Paso Tombstone Pink, Paso Tombstone Red, Mortal Zin, Dark Phantom & Deliverance are priced for everyday enjoyment. Or as the owners say they are priced to allow you to "Drink in Peace".

The views from the hilltop winery are breathtaking with plenty of room for picnicking, fishing in the pond & enjoying a stroll through the vineyards.

CURIOUS NAME, SERIOUS WINE!

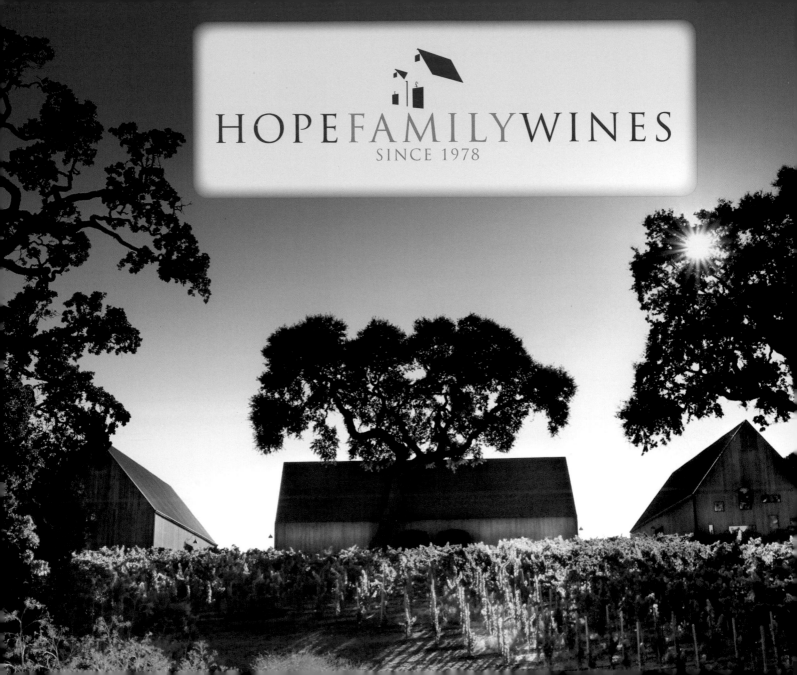

Hope Family Wines
Party Spread

When entertaining large crowds it is nice to give people a choice of several different wines, a wide range of flavors and food they can nibble on all evening long. Open the wine and let the party begin!

The Wine Bar

Treana White - the name symbolizes a trio of natural elements that directly and positively influence the wine: the sun, the soil and the sea

Troublemaker - the name of this Rhône-based blend defines both the wine and its maker

Candor Zinfandel - multi-vintage and varietally correct

Austin Hope Grenache - beautiful estate-grown artisan wine

Liberty School Cabernet Sauvignon - delicious, fruit-driven and approachable

The Food Table

Paté with French Bread p26
Butternut Squash Dip with Blue Corn Chips p12
Hummus with Pita Crisps and Raw Vegetables p15
Smoked Salmon Puffs p24
Beef, Chicken and Tofu Satay p57
Spicy Pork Meatballs p27
Beef Sliders p61
Dried Fruit, Nuts and Cheese Platter

The Hope family arrived in Paso Robles in 1978 in search of land and new opportunities. They were among a handful of pioneering families who helped shape and gain recognition for this distinctive winegrowning region.

After growing grapes and developing vineyards throughout the eighties and early nineties, they began producing estate wines under the Hope Farms label. Over time it has become abundantly clear to the Hope family that Paso Robles is capable of producing world-class wines. Today, as Hope Family Wines, the winery crafts elegant wines under five diverse labels: Treana, Austin Hope, Troublemaker, Liberty School and Candor.

Tasting Room Open
Friday & Saturday 10am - 4pm
Thursday by Appointment

1585 Live Oak Road, Paso Robles
805.238.4112   hfwines.com

Open Thurs–Sun, 12am – 5pm
or by appointment
2525 Mitchell Ranch Way, Paso Robles
(between Robert Hall and Vina Robles)

805.239.8555   mitchella.com

Garden Luncheon

This menu was created by Mitchella Vineyard & Winery to be enjoyed in a peaceful garden setting. Mitchella often wins first place for their recipes at the annual Paso Robles Winemaker Cook-off...try these to impress your friends!

Grilled Shrimp Caesar p73
Mitchella Viognier

Petite Top Sirlion Burgers with Rustic Cheddar, Caramelized Onions and Heirloom Tomatoes p61
Mitchella Shameless - an estate blend of Grenache, Mourvèdre and Syrah

Fresh Peach Cobbler p177
Mitchella Riportella Bianco

"Life is an Adventure, Drink Wine"™

Since 1997, Darren and Angela Mitchell have been committed to making small lots of premium handcrafted wines from their family owned estate vineyard and winery. They believe it starts by attentively cultivating quality wine in the vineyard, proudly located in the rolling hills east of Paso Robles, their 20 acre vineyard is planted with Cabernet Sauvignon, Syrah, Mourvèdre, Grenache, and Portuguese grape varietals Tinto Cao and Touriga Nacional.

Currently, Mitchella produces 1,500 cases annually, anything that is not estate grown is sourced from the best vineyards in the Paso Robles AVA. It is the owners' ambition to make only the finest wines and to remain a small winery; producing no more than 5,000 cases per year. You will only find their wines at the winery or in select wine bars, shops and restaurants in California.

Nestled among the vines with splendid views of Paso Robles their tasting room is welcoming and relaxing.

Pear Valley

Pear Valley

Sunday Supper

Cozy up around the table and savor the flavors of this four course dinner. Perfect with friends, family or that extra special someone.

Salmon Petals p21
Pear Valley Chardonnay

White Bean & Sausage Soup p97
Pear Valley Syrah

Garlic Stuffed Pork Roast p124
with Sweet Potato Fries and Green Beans
Pear Valley "Distraction"

Dark Chocolate Pie p187
topped with Cream and Stawberries
Pear Valley Orange Muscat

Pear Valley is Tom and Kathleen Maas' family winery designed to make visitors feel welcome.

Selecting from over 20 grape varietals grown on their estate vineyards, they create unique vintages that reflect the vibrant fruit nourished by ancient soils while leaving little impact on the environment. The Maas family cordially offers novice wine drinkers, enthusiasts and connoisseurs a taste of the naturally good life captured in each bottle of Pear Valley wine.

Visit the tasting room and enjoy the 360 degree views of Paso Robles countryside while sipping Pear Valley wine. Bring a picnic, sit back and relax while enjoying the soft music piped throughout the picnic area.

Open Daily 11am - 5pm
4900 Union Road, Paso Robles
805.237.2861   pearvalley.com

Open Friday - Sunday
11am-5pm
13350 River Road, San Miguel
805.467.3104   prettysmith.com

PRETTY SMITH

Vineyards & Winery

A Culinary Adventure

Exploring new foods can be a lot of fun!
Try this menu for a unique dining experience.

Sautéed Frogs Legs p59
served on a bed of Asian Slaw p66
Pretty-Smith Sauvignon Blanc

Grilled Chevon p155
served with Soba Noodles p125
and Stir-fried Vegetables p147
Pretty-Smith Palette de Rouge, an estate blend
of Cabernet Sauvignon, Cabernet Franc, Merlot and Malbec

Baklava with a Grilled Peach 179
Pretty-Smith Zinfandel Port (tawny style)

Pretty-Smith Vineyards & Winery is a one woman operation producing 100% estate-grown fruit under the Pretty-Smith label. The line-up includes a number of stand alone varietals as well as the signature wine, a blend known as Palette de Rouge. The red wines are aged in oak for 3.5 years and bottle aged for an additional year prior to release to create a SOFT, SMOOTH and SILKY style.

The estate property offers wonderful views of the surrounding vineyards and the hills of San Miguel. Bring a picnic lunch or plan ahead and reserve the Pretty Café -- Pretty-Smith's private event room. Lisa Pretty will develop a custom wine-paired menu for groups of six people or more. The Pretty Café is able to accomodate 36 people seated inside and 24 outside on the deck, making it the ideal venue for intimate dinners or special events.

Kokopelli awaits!

Ranchita Canyon Vineyard
Winemaker's Dinner

This comforting menu is great to share with family and friends. Continue to sip a little Port after dessert and enjoy an evening full of conversation.

Eggplant Rollups p34
Ranchita Canyon Sangiovese

Cream of Mushroom Soup p91
Ranchita Canyon Petit Verdot

Spicy Beef Ribs served with p133
Mashed Potatoes and Green Beans
Ranchita Canyon Old Vine Petite Sirah

Chocolate Cheesecake p181
topped with Port Soaked Stawberries
Ranchita Canyon Cabernet Sauvignon "Port"

Ranchita Canyon Vineyard is a family owned and operated vineyard and boutique winery on the hills overlooking beautiful Pleasant Valley. Come visit and meet owners Bill, Teresa, & their teenagers Adam and Anna, who all work together to produce estate grown, small lot handcrafted wines. The hillside location is great for growing premium wine grapes, and provides beautiful views as you enjoy your picnic on our new deck/patio area. The vineyard was founded in 1970, and they still produce wine from the old vine Zinfandel & Petite Sirah. Ten different varieties are planted, so they have a wine for every occasion. Visit Ranchita Canyon Vineyard, and enjoy the beauty, serenity, and fine wines.

Open
Fri-Mon 11am-5pm

3439 Ranchita Canyon
San Miguel, CA
805.467.9448

Ranchita Canyon
VINEYARD

ranchitacanyonvineyard.com

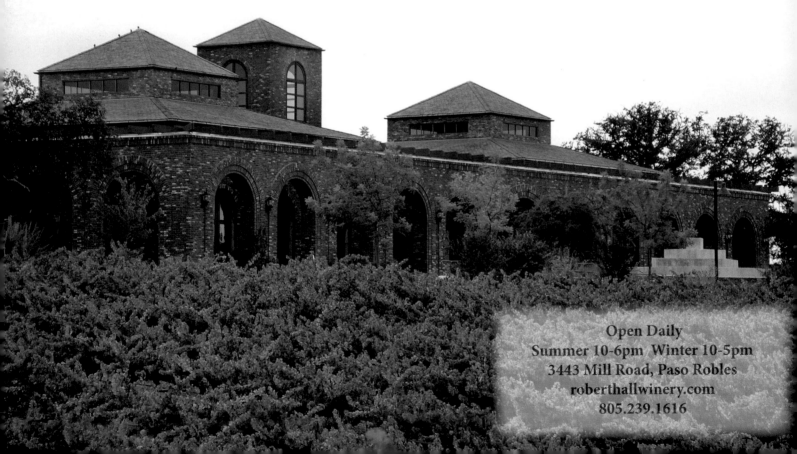

ROBERT HALL WINERY
"The Essence of Paso Robles"

Open Daily
Summer 10-6pm Winter 10-5pm
3443 Mill Road, Paso Robles
roberthallwinery.com
805.239.1616

Robert Hall
Winemaker's Dinner

As you enjoy this five course meal with Robert Hall wines you will see why they were the first Central Coast winery to receive the Golden State Winery award.

Shrimp Rolls p53
Robert Hall Sauvignon Blanc

Spinach & Strawberry Salad p80
Robert Hall Viognier

Potato Leek Soup p95
Robert Hall Chardonnay

Grilled Ribeye Steak with Root Vegetables p148
Robert Hall Cabernet Sauvignon

Vanilla Crème Brûlée p171
Robert Hall Orange Muscat

"The Essence of Paso Robles"™

At Robert Hall time-tested techniques and practices are used to cultivate intensely colored and flavored Paso Robles grapes. In the winery the grapes are crafted into rich wines that capture the essence of Paso Robles. This craftsmanship in concert with an accessible, inviting facility provides a superior wine experience for visitors.

Paso Robles has a reputation for producing superior reds, especially, Cabernet Sauvignon and Rhône varietals. Robert Hall Winery has made a commitment to the production of Rhone wines, with a portfolio that includes Viognier, a white-Rhone blend Blanc de Robles, a dry-rosé Rosé de Robles, the red-Rhone blends Rhone de Robles and Pape de Robles, Grenache, Syrah and Petite Sirah. The portfolio also includes a traditional set of Cabernet Sauvignon, Cabernet Franc, Merlot, Chardonnay and Sauvignon Blanc, in addition to their Meritage – a classic blend of Cabernet Sauvignon, Cabernet Franc, Malbec and Merlot. A traditional Vintage Port, and an Orange Muscat round out the family of wines.

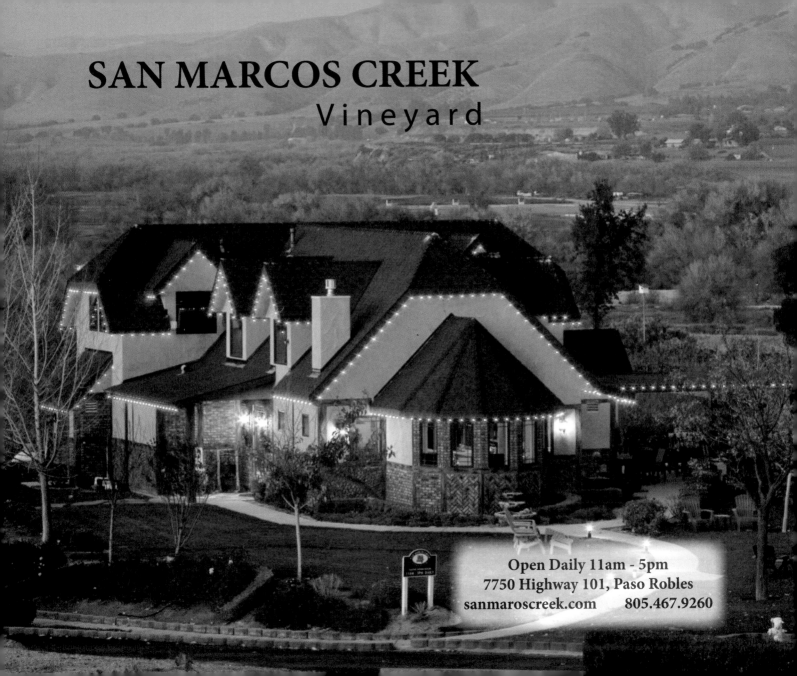

SAN MARCOS CREEK
Vineyard

Open Daily 11am - 5pm
7750 Highway 101, Paso Robles
sanmaroscreek.com   805.467.9260

SAN MARCOS CREEK
Vineyard

Harvest Afternoon BBQ

With the beautiful setting at San Marcos Creek, an outdoor meal with plenty of grilled food is a family favorite after a day harvesting grapes.

Grilled Eggplant Roll-ups p34
San Marcos Creek White Merlot

Grilled Portabella Mushrooms p38
San Marcos Creek Red Table Wine

Blue Cheese Stuffed Steak p137
with grilled vegetables and grilled flatbread
San Marcos Creek Zinfandel

Port Soaked Grilled Peaches
served with Vanilla Ice Cream
San Marcos Creek Late Harvest Zinfandel

High school sweethearts for over fifty short years, Fling and Annette Traylor journeyed up the coast from their home in Southern California in search of a slower, gentler pace of life. In Paso Robles they found their dream in the form of a sheep ranch just a bit north of town, directly on historic Highway 101. Annette fell in love with the beauty of the property, but was not very fond of the sheep... Fling's dream suddenly become a bit clearer..."perhaps a vineyard would be a nice retirement activity..."

Fling and Annette planted 40 acres of premium grapes and established grower contracts with several prestigious local wineries. With the success of their retirement dream, Fling and Annette were also able to realize another dream, that of developing a family business. Daughter, Catherine, and her husband, Brady Winter joined the business in 2002 when they too moved up from Southern California and were instrumental in starting the Winery and Tasting Room. Most every day of the week you will find either Brady or Cathy (and some times both!) in the tasting room, pouring their fine award winning wines for your pleasure.

SILVER HORSE

Silver Horse
Pizza Party

Silver Horse fires up the pizza oven once a month for their Funday Sunday parties. Steve Kroener's pizzas draw a crowd and here is his menu for the perfect pizza party.

Japhen Chopped Salad p67
Silver Horse Albariño

Sausage Rolls p30
Silver Horse Tomori, a blend of Syrah and Cabernet Sauvignon

Pizza Margerita p40
Silver Horse The Big Easy , a blend of Malbec, Cabernet Sauvignon, Merlot, and Petite Sirah

Pizza Bianco p40
Silver Horse Tempranillo

SOZINHO Chocolate Cake p185
Silver Horse Sozinho Port

Silver Horse Vineyard got its start in 1989 when most of the grapes on the property were planted. In 1997, the Kroener family came on the scene. Jim and Suzanna Kroener have always loved wine; in fact, Jim's father made it back home in Los Angeles. The vineyard was thriving with premium grapes and they decided to build a new winery and hospitality center to create handcrafted wines from their Bordeaux and Spanish grape varietals. The Kroener's son, Steve, came on the scene to help with the family business. Today he makes food-friendly wines, as his Grandfather had years before, that are age worthy and varietally correct. Be sure to try his unique blends.

The tasting room, event facility, picnic area, bocce ball courts and horse shoe pits offer beautiful views of the surrounding Pleasant Valley area that encourage visitors to linger and enjoy. The Kroeners are more than willing to share…hence the statement on the back of every bottle "Not For Us Alone".

*Open Friday-Sunday 11am - 5pm
2995 Pleasant Road, San Miguel
805.467.WINE   silverhorse.com*

TABLAS
CREEK
VINEYARD

TABLAS CREEK
VINEYARD

Classic Pairings

Tablas Creek flagship wines paired with some classic,
Provençal menu items.

Crab Orzo Salad p82
Tablas Creek Esprit de Beaucastel Blanc, the flagship white
Rhône blend of Roussanne, Grenache Blanc and Picpoul Blanc

Grilled Salmon p108
with Mediterranean Quinoa p157
Tablas Creek Rosé, a dry blend of Mourvèdre,
Grenache and Counoise

Braised Lamb Shank p127
served with Roasted Potatoes
Tablas Creek Esprit de Beaucastel, the flagship red Rhône
blend of Mourvèdre, Grenache, Syrah and Counoise

Baked Apples p166
Tablas Creek Vin de Paille

Tablas Creek Vineyard was founded by the Perrin family of Château de Beaucastel and importer Robert Haas. They chose the hilly Las Tablas district of west Paso Robles for its similarities to Châteauneuf du Pape: limestone soils, a favorable climate, and rugged terrain.

The partners imported the traditional varietals grown on the Perrins' celebrated estate, reproduced them on-site, and planted them in their organically farmed estate vineyard. Tablas Creek follows the Châteauneuf du Pape tradition of blending to produce wines of balance and elegance.

The vineyard's signature wines, designed for long aging, are the Esprit de Beaucastel and Esprit de Beaucastel Blanc. The Côtes de Tablas and Côtes de Tablas Blanc show lush, rich flavors, while the Patelin de Tablas and Patelin de Tablas Blanc are fresh, clean and bright.

Open Daily 10am - 5pm
9339 Adelaida Road, Paso Robles
805.237.1231   tablascreek.com

~221~

Tobin James
Summer Menu

Chef Marc LeDuc
*This menu is especially perfect al fresco
with a beautiful Paso sunset.*

Chilled Roasted Garlic and Almond Soup p88
James Gang Reserve Chardonnay

Organic Tomato and Herb Flatbread p17
Tobin James Primo Sangiovese

Ballistic Zinfandel Braised Lamb Shank p131
Tobin James Ballistic Zinfandel

Liquid Love Blackberry Snow p165
Tobin James Liquid Love Late Harvest Zinfandel

A visit to Tobin James Cellars—always one of Paso Robles' most popular wineries and tasting rooms—will give you a good idea of what Paso Robles is all about. Family owned and operated since 1987, the winery's friendly, saloon-style tasting room offers a nod to the area's Western heritage, while the winery's outstanding wines show why Paso Robles is being celebrated as a premium wine producing area. Tobin James wines boast true "Paso Robles in a Glass" character with intense varietal flavors, true to the appellation. The legendary eleven different Zinfandels, the stellar world class Syrahs, Chardonnays, Cabernet Sauvignons, and Meritage blends reflect the Tobin James philosophy of Winemaking: Balanced complex wines with luscious intense fruit.

Visit Tobin James Cellars and taste all of your favorite wines at the grand, ornate 1860's antique Brunswick bar where Jesse James himself would "belly-up." You'll come for the wines and stay for the fun or vice versa! Bring your picnic to enjoy in the beautiful mosaic outdoor grotto.

Vina Robles

Open Daily
Summer 10-6pm   Winter 10-5pm
3700 Mill Road, Paso Robles
vinarobles.com   805.227.4812

Vina Robles
Mediterranean Inspired Menu

Bring Vina Robles' winemaking philosophy of combining the best of the Old and New worlds to your very own dinner table. Each dish is based on a traditional recipe but prepared with a modern twist and fresh flavors, which will complement the wines and enhance your overall dining experience.

Smoked Salmon Puffs p24
Vina Robles Sauvignon Blanc

Polenta Rounds p35
served on a bed of greens
Vina Robles Red[4] - A powerful Rhône-style blend of Syrah, Petite Sirah, Grenache, and Mourvèdre. Serve chilled.

Lamb Kabobs p129
served with grilled vegetables p149
and Gorgonzola/Spinach Risotto p157
Vina Robles Signature - A rich and full-bodied Petit Verdot based blend with dark fruit aromas and ripe, silky tannins.

Chocolate Crème Brûlée p171
topped with wine soaked raspberries
Vina Robles Petite Sirah

European Inspiration – California Character

Vina Robles crafts wines that represent a stylistic bridge between the Old and New worlds, capturing the finesse associated with European wines while celebrating the bold natural flavors of their estate vineyards in Paso Robles. Here, proprietor Hans Nef and managing partner Hans – R. Michel bring their Swiss heritage to California's Central Coast, where they aim to unite the best of both experiences.

Vina Robles specializes in varieties that excel in the complex soils and nuanced microclimates of Paso Robles, including Cabernet Sauvignon, Petit Verdot, Syrah, Petite Sirah, and Sauvignon Blanc. They also embrace unconventional blends as an opportunity to create wines of distinctive quality and character.

The wines are available across the United States and overseas, and can be enjoyed at the hospitality center in the heart of Paso Robles wine country. Visit soon to experience the Vina Robles difference and enjoy gracious hospitality, beautiful grounds, and fine art.

WILD HORSE
WINERY & VINEYARDS

Unbridled Dinner

Unbridled and unbelievably delicious, this menu will tantalize your guests' taste buds.

Crab Louis p81
Wild Horse Verdelho

Salmon Bisque p94
Wild Horse Unbridled Chardonnay (Bien Nacido Vineyard)

Wild Mushroom & Goat Cheese Tart p37
Wild Horse Unbridled Pinot Noir (Bien Nacido Vineyard)

Beef Stroganoff p138
Wild Horse Unbridled Merlot

At Wild Horse Winery & Vineyards, the free-spirited attitude, driving curiosity and passion for fine winemaking are what make them unique.

Located south of Paso Robles, in Templeton, California, Wild Horse Winery & Vineyards creates compelling wines from 16 diverse appellations and more than 50 vineyards from the Central Coast. "Live Naturally, Enjoy Wildly" reflects the attitude and personalities of the people who have been creating these wines for over 25 years.

Open Daily 11am to 5pm
1437 Wild Horse Winery Ct.
Templeton, CA 93465

805.788.6310

wildhorsewinery.com

WINDWARD
VINEYARD

A Harvest Menu for All Seasons

Marc and Maggie produce exclusively Pinot Noir -- here is their menu to showcase their food friendly wine.

Shitake Bacon Salad p79
Windward Vineyard Estate Pinot Noir

Schiacciata con uva p18
Windward Vineyard Estate Pinot Noir

Duck Paella with Mushrooms p116
Windward Vineyard Estate Pinot Noir GOLD Barrel Select

Rustic Nut Tart p173
Windward Vineyard Estate Pinot Noir

"Exclusively Pinot Noir" is the hallmark of Windward Vineyard. Owners/operators Marc Goldberg and Maggie D'Ambrosia specialize in 100% Estate-grown and produced Burgundian-style, handcrafted Pinot Noir.

Named for the cool Pacific Ocean winds that breeze through the Templeton Gap in the Santa Lucia Mountain Chain, on the Westside of Paso Robles, Windward Vineyard Pinot Noir is testimony to the unique microclimate and terroir of the area.

Visit the tasting room for a vertical tasting of four vintages of Pinot Noir along with the Café Menu of artisan cheeses and salamis available 7 days a week. Enjoy a glass or bottle in the peaceful Lath House overlooking the vineyard or while playing a game of Bocce Ball.

Open Daily
10:30am - 5:00pm
1380 Live Oak Road, Paso Robles "Westside"
805.239.2565 windwardvineyard.com

Paso Robles Wines
from A to Z

While most people are familar with the common grape varietals like Chardonnay, Cabernet Sauvignon, Syrah and Zinfandel, there are a growing number of the more unusual grapes such as Aglianico, Blaufrankish, Counoise, Lagrein, Refosco and Verdelho being produced in Paso Robles. This Appendix lists all the wines I could find from A to Z along with the wineries that produce them.

The wines and producers are listed in alphabetical order. White wines are in green, rosés in pink, sherries in orange and reds in a dark burgundy.

I would like to say I found every winery and every wine; however, with over 200 bonded wineries in Paso Robles it is extremely difficult to keep up with what every one is doing. A large portion of the data found in this chapter was obtained from the Paso Robles Wine Country Alliance (pasowine.com) and since their data base is updated every year I recommend you look there if there is a wine or a producer you can't find.

Aglianico
Caparone Winery
Kenneth Volk Vineyards
Locatelli Vineyards & Winery
Via Vega Winery
Villa Creek Cellars

Albariño
Arroyo Robles Winery
Bodegas M
Bodegas paso Robles
Chronic Cellars Winery Inc.
JK Wine Company
Lone Madrone
Moonstone Cellars
RN Estate Vineyard & Winery
Silver Horse Winery

Arneis
August Ridge Vineyards

Barbera
August Ridge Vineyards
Bella Luna Winery
Christian Lazo Wines
Chumeia Vineyards
Doce Robles Winery
Eberle Winery
Fratelli Perata

Hunt Cellars
J&J Cellars
Locatelli Vineyards & Winery
Lone Madrone
Nadeau Family Vintners
Niner Wine Estates
Norman Vineyards
Opolo Vineyards
Pianetta Winery
Tobin James Cellars
Vista Del Rey Vineyards

Blaufrankish
Wild Horse Winery & Vineyards

Bordeaux Blend
Asuncion Ridge
Ancient Peaks Winery
Arroyo Robles Winery
B & E Vineyard/Winery
Calcareous Vineyard
Cerro Prieto Vineyard and Cellars
Changala Winery
Christian Lazo Wines
Cinquain Cellars
Clayhouse Wines
Cypher Winery
DAOU Vineyards
Dark Star Cellars
Derby Wine Estates

Ecluse Wines
Eos Estate Winery
GreMarK Vineyards
Grey Wolf Vineyards & Cellars
Halter Ranch Vineyard
HammerSky Vineyards
Harmony Cellars
Hidden Oak Winery
Hug Cellars
Hunt Cellars
J. Lohr Vineyards & Wines
Jada Vineyard & Winery
JUSTIN Vineyards & Winery
Kiamie Wine Cellars
Le Vigne Winery
Maloy O'Neill Vineyards
Midnight Cellars
Minassian-Young Vineyards
Mondo Cellars
Moonstone Cellars
Niner Wine Estates
Opolo Vineyards
Oso Libre Winery
Parrish Family Vineyard
Peachy Canyon Winery
Pear Valley Vineyard
Per Cazo Cellars
Pozo Valley
Pretty-Smith Vineyards & Winery
Proulx

Ranchita Canyon Vineyard
Robert Hall Winery
Sextant Wines
Stacked Stone Cellars
Starr Ranch Vineyards and Winery
Still Waters Vineyards
Summerwood Winery
Victor Hugo Winery
Villicana Winery
Vina Robles
Zenaida Cellars

Cabernet Franc

Adelaida Cellars
Ancient Peaks Winery
Anglim Winery
B & E Vineyard/Winery
Bianchi Winery
Calcareous Vineyard
Carmody McKnight Estate Wines
Cass Winery
Castoro Cellars
Chateau Margene
Clautiere Vineyard
Dark Star Cellars
Derby Wine Estates
Doce Robles Winery
Dunning Vineyards Estate Winery
Fratelli Perata
Frolicking Frog

Halter Ranch Vineyard
HammerSky Vineyards
Hearst Ranch Winery
Hunt Cellars
JK Wine Company
Kenneth Volk Vineyards
Le Vigne Winery
Maloy O'Neill Vineyards
Midnight Cellars
Mitchella Vineyard & Winery
Moonstone Cellars
Nichols Winery & Cellars
Niner Wine Estates
Opolo Vineyards
Peachy Canyon Winery
Pear Valley Vineyard
Pretty-Smith Vineyards & Winery
Proulx
Ranchita Canyon Vineyard
Rangeland Wines
RN Estate Vineyard & Winery
Robert Hall Winery
Rotta Winery
San Marcos Creek Vineyard
Starr Ranch Vineyards and Winery
Still Waters Vineyards
Via Vega Winery
Tobin James Cellars
Wild Horse Winery & Vineyards

Cabernet Sauvignon

Adelaida Cellars
Ancient Peaks Winery
Anglim Winery
AronHill Vineyards
Arroyo Robles Winery
August Ridge Vineyards
B & E Vineyard/Winery
Bear Cave Cellars
Bianchi Winery
Bishop's Peak
Brochelle Vineyards
Calcareous Vineyard
Caliza Winery
Caparone Winery
Carina Cellars
Carmody McKnight Estate Wines
Cass Winery
Cayucos Cellars
Cerro Prieto Vineyard and Cellars
Changala Winery
Chateau Margene
Chumeia Vineyards
Clautiere Vineyard
Clayhouse Wines
D'Anbino Vineyards & Cellars
DAOU Vineyards
Dark Star Cellars
Derby Wine Estates
Doce Robles Winery

Donatoni Winery
Dover Canyon Winery
Dunning Vineyards Estate Winery
Eberle Winery
Ecluse Wines
Eos Estate Winery
Falcon Nest Winery
Fratelli Perata
Frolicking Frog
FS Cellars
Gelfand Vineyards
Graveyard Vineyards
GreMarK Vineyards
Grey Wolf Vineyards & Cellars
Halter Ranch Vineyard
Hansen Winery
Harmony Cellars
Hearst Ranch Winery
Hearthstone Vineyard & Winery
Hug Cellars
Hunt Cellars
J&J Cellars
J. Lohr Vineyards & Wines
JK Wine Company
JUSTIN Vineyards & Winery
Kenneth Volk Vineyards
Kiamie Wine Cellars
L'Aventure Winery
Laraneta Winery
Le Vigne Winery

Locatelli Vineyards & Winery
Lone Madrone
Madison Cellars
Maloy O'Neill Vineyards
Meridian Vineyards
Midnight Cellars
Minassian-Young Vineyards
Mitchella Vineyard & Winery
Moonstone Cellars
Nadeau Family Vintners
Nichols Winery & Cellars
Niner Wine Estates
Norman Vineyards
Opolo Vineyards
Ortman Family Wines
Oso Libre Winery
Parrish Family Vineyard
Peachy Canyon Winery
Pear Valley Vineyard
Penman Springs Vineyard
Pianetta Winery
Poalillo Vineyards
Pomar Junction Vineyard & Winery
Pozo Valley
Pretty-Smith Vineyards & Winery
Proulx
Rabbit Ridge Winery
Ranchita Canyon Vineyard
Rangeland Wines
Red Soles Winery

Riverstar Vineyards
RN Estate Vineyard & Winery
Robert Hall Winery
Rocky Creek Cellars
Rotta Winery
San Marcos Creek Vineyard
Sarzotti Winery
Sculpterra Winery
Silver Horse Winery
STANGER
Starr Ranch Vineyards and Winery
Steinbeck Vineyards & Winery
Stephen's Cellar
Still Waters Vineyards
Summerwood Winery
Tackitt Family Vineyards
Tobin James Cellars
Tolo Cellars
Treana and Hope Family Wines
Twilight Cellars
Venteux Vineyards
Veris Cellars
Via Vega Winery
Victor Hugo Winery
Villa San Juliette
Villicana Winery
Vina Robles
Wild Horse Winery & Vineyards
Zenaida Cellars

Charbono

Castoro Cellars
Fratelli Perata
Pear Valley Vineyard
Turley Wine Cellars

Chardonnay

Adelaida Cellars
Arroyo Robles Winery
Bianchi Winery
Bishop's Peak
Calcareous Vineyard
Carmody McKnight Estate Wines
Castoro Cellars
Cayucos Cellars
Chumeia Vineyards
Cinquain Cellars
CrossLynn Estate
Cypher Winery
DAOU Vineyards
Donatoni Winery
Dunning Vineyards Estate Winery
Eberle Winery
Eos Estate Winery
FS Cellars
Harmony Cellars
Hearst Ranch Winery
Hunt Cellars
J&J Cellars
J. Lohr Vineyards & Wines

Jack Creek Cellars
JUSTIN Vineyards & Winery
Kenneth Volk Vineyards
Le Cuvier
Le Vigne Winery
Maloy O'Neill Vineyards
Meridian Vineyards
Midnight Cellars
Mitchella Vineyard & Winery
Moonstone Cellars
Nadeau Family Vintners
Norman Vineyards
Opolo Vineyards
Ortman Family Wines
Oso Libre Winery
Parrish Family Vineyard
Pear Valley Vineyard
Pithy Little Wine Company
Poalillo Vineyards
Pomar Junction Vineyard & Winery
Proulx
Rabbit Ridge Winery
Red Soles Winery
Robert Hall Winery
Rotta Winery
Sarzotti Winery
Sculpterra Winery
Sextant Wines
STANGER
Stephen's Cellar

Still Waters Vineyards
Summerwood Winery
Tablas Creek Vineyard
Tassajara Cellars
Tobin James Cellars
Treana and Hope Family Wines
Twilight Cellars
Veris Cellars
Vina Robles
Westberg Cellars
Wild Horse Winery & Vineyards
Zenaida Cellars

Chenin Blanc

Clayhouse Wines

Counoise

Adelaida Cellars
Clautiere Vineyard
Derby Wine Estates
Edward Sellers Vineyards & Wines
Opolo Vineyards
Tablas Creek Vineyard
Terry Hoage Vineyards

Dessert Sherry

Rotta Winery

Dessert Wine

Anglim Winery
AronHill Vineyards
Arroyo Robles Winery
Carmody McKnight Estate Wines
Chronic Cellars Winery Inc.
Clayhouse Wines
D'Anbino Vineyards & Cellars
Eos Estate Winery
Halter Ranch Vineyard
Hearst Ranch Winery
Hunt Cellars
Le Vigne Winery
Locatelli Vineyards & Winery
Lone Madrone
Meridian Vineyards
Mitchella Vineyard & Winery
Moonstone Cellars
Opolo Vineyards
Oso Libre Winery
PasoPort Wine Company Inc.
Peachy Canyon Winery
Pear Valley Vineyard
Ranchita Canyon Vineyard
Riverstar Vineyards
Sarzotti Winery
STANGER
Stephen's Cellar
Still Waters Vineyards
Tablas Creek Vineyard

Tackitt Family Vineyards
Twilight Cellars

Dolcetto

August Ridge Vineyards
Tobin James Cellars

Gamay

Adelaida Cellars

Gewurztraminer

Castoro Cellars
Eos Estate Winery
Meridian Vineyards
Minassian-Young Vineyards
Moonstone Cellars
Tackitt Family Vineyards

Grenache

Alta Colina Vineyard & Winery
AmByth Estate
Anglim Winery
Arroyo Robles Winery
Barrel 27 Wine Company
Calcareous Vineyard
Caliza Winery
Carina Cellars
Cass Winery
Changala Winery

Chronic Cellars Winery Inc.
Clautiere Vineyard
Croad Vineyards
CrossLynn Estate
Cypher Winery
Denner Vineyards
Dover Canyon Winery
Edward Sellers Vineyards & Wines
Grey Wolf Vineyards & Cellars
Halter Ranch Vineyard
Hearthstone Vineyard & Winery
Herman Story Wines
Hug Cellars
JK Wine Company
Kaleidos
Kenneth Volk Vineyards
Linne Calodo Cellars
Lone Madrone
Minassian-Young Vineyards
Mitchella Vineyard & Winery
Nadeau Family Vintners
Opolo Vineyards
Oso Libre Winery
Orchid Hill Vineyard
Per Cazo Cellars
Pipestone Vineyards
Proulx
Robert Hall Winery
Summerwood Winery
Tablas Creek Vineyard

Tassajara Cellars
Terry Hoage Vineyards
Treana and Hope Family Wines
Twilight Cellars
Venteux Vineyards
Via Vega Winery
Villa Creek Cellars
Villicana Winery
Zenaida Cellars

Grenache Blanc
Adelaida Cellars
Alta Colina Vineyard & Winery
AmByth Estate
Anglim Winery
Caliza Winery
Chronic Cellars Winery Inc.
Clavo Cellars
Clayhouse Wines
Cypher Winery
Edward Sellers Vineyards & Wines
Eos Estate Winery
Grey Wolf Vineyards & Cellars
JK Wine Company
Lone Madrone
Per Cazo Cellars
Proulx
Ranchita Canyon Vineyard
Tablas Creek Vineyard
Tassajara Cellars

Terry Hoage Vineyards
Twilight Cellars
Villa Creek Cellars
Villa San Juliette

Lagrein
Maloy O'Neill Vineyards
Tobin James Cellars

Malbec
Ancient Peaks Winery
Changala Winery
Cinquain Cellars
Clautiere Vineyard
Clayhouse Wines
Cypher Winery
Eos Estate Winery
Halter Ranch Vineyard
Hansen Winery
Harmony Cellars
Hearst Ranch Winery
J&J Cellars
JUSTIN Vineyards & Winery
Locatelli Vineyards & Winery
Maloy O'Neill Vineyards
Midnight Cellars
Minassian-Young Vineyards
Opolo Vineyards
Peachy Canyon Winery
Pear Valley Vineyard

Pretty-Smith Vineyards & Winery
Ranchita Canyon Vineyard
Silver Horse Winery
Still Waters Vineyards
Via Vega Winery
Victor Hugo Winery
Wild Horse Winery & Vineyards

Malvasia Bianca
Bodega Paso Robles
Kenneth Volk Vineyards
Pithy Little Wine Company
Wild Horse Winery & Vineyards

Marsanne
Alta Colina Vineyard & Winery
AmByth Estate
Anglim Winery
Barrel 27 Wine Company
Calcareous Vineyard
Changala Winery
Chronic Cellars Winery Inc.
Edward Sellers Vineyards & Wines
Eos Estate Winery
Grey Wolf Vineyards & Cellars
JK Wine Company
Proulx
Venteux Vineyards

Merlot

Ancient Peaks Winery
Arroyo Robles Winery
August Ridge Vineyards
B & E Vineyard/Winery
Bianchi Winery
Caparone Winery
Carmody McKnight Estate Wines
Castoro Cellars
Cerro Prieto Vineyard and Cellars
Chumeia Vineyards
Cinquain Cellars
DAOU Vineyards
Dark Star Cellars
Doce Robles Winery
Eos Estate Winery
Falcon Nest Winery
Fratelli Perata
Frolicking Frog
Halter Ranch Vineyard
HammerSky Vineyards
Hansen Winery
Harmony Cellars
Hearst Ranch Winery
Hidden Oak Winery
Hunt Cellars
J&J Cellars
J. Lohr Vineyards & Wines
Kenneth Volk Vineyards
Laraneta Winery

Le Vigne Winery
Madison Cellars
Maloy O'Neill Vineyards
Meridian Vineyards
Midnight Cellars
Moonstone Cellars
Nichols Winery & Cellars
Niner Wine Estates
Norman Vineyards
Opolo Vineyards
Peachy Canyon Winery
Pear Valley Vineyard
Penman Springs Vineyard
Pithy Little Wine Company
Pomar Junction Vineyard & Winery
Pozo Valley
Proulx
Rabbit Ridge Winery
Ranchita Canyon Vineyard
Rangeland Wines
Riverstar Vineyards
RN Estate Vineyard & Winery
Robert Hall Winery
Rocky Creek Cellars
Rotta Winery
San Marcos Creek Vineyard
Sarzotti Winery
Silver Horse Winery
Still Waters Vineyards
Summerwood Winery

Tackitt Family Vineyards
Tobin James Cellars
Treana and Hope Family Wines
Twilight Cellars
Veris Cellars
Via Vega Winery
Victor Hugo Winery
Villa San Juliette
Villicana Winery
Wild Coyote Estate Winery
Wild Horse Winery & Vineyards

Mourvedre

Adelaida Cellars
Alta Colina Vineyard & Winery
AmByth Estate
Anglim Winery
Arroyo Robles Winery
Calcareous Vineyard
Caliza Winery
Carina Cellars
Cass Winery
Chronic Cellars Winery Inc.
Clautiere Vineyard
Croad Vineyards
Cypher Winery
Derby Wine Estates
Edward Sellers Vineyards & Wines
FS Cellars
Grey Wolf Vineyards & Cellars

Hug Cellars
J. Lohr Vineyards & Wines
JK Wine Company
Kenneth Volk Vineyards
Linne Calodo Cellars
Lone Madrone
Minassian-Young Vineyards
Mitchella Vineyard & Winery
Nadeau Family Vintners
Opolo Vineyards
Oso Libre Winery
Pipestone Vineyards
Proulx
Rangeland Wines
RN Estate Vineyard & Winery
Tablas Creek Vineyard
Tassajara Cellars
Terry Hoage Vineyards
Thacher Winery
Twilight Cellars
Venteux Vineyards
Villa Creek Cellars
Villicana Winery

Nebbiolo
AJB Vineyards
August Ridge Vineyards
Berardo Vineyards and Winery
Caparone Winery
Lone Madrone

Opolo Vineyards
San Marcos Creek Vineyard

Négrette
Kenneth Volk Vineyards
Wild Horse Winery & Vineyards

Orange Muscat
B & E Vineyard/Winery
J&J Cellars
JUSTIN Vineyards & Winery
Kenneth Volk Vineyards
Pear Valley Vineyard
Robert Hall Winery

Petit Verdot
Ancient Peaks Winery
Barrel 27 Wine Company
Calcareous Vineyard
Castoro Cellars
Changala Winery
Clautiere Vineyard
Clayhouse Wines
Cypher Winery
Eos Estate Winery
Fratelli Perata
Grey Wolf Vineyards & Cellars
HammerSky Vineyards
J&J Cellars
JK Wine Company

JUSTIN Vineyards & Winery
Midnight Cellars
Opolo Vineyards
Peachy Canyon Winery
Penman Springs Vineyard
Ranchita Canyon Vineyard
Rangeland Wines
Silver Horse Winery
Tackitt Family Vineyards
Tolo Cellars
Twilight Cellars
Vina Robles

Petite Sirah
Alta Colina Vineyard & Winery
Ancient Peaks Winery
Anglim Winery
Arroyo Robles Winery
Bianchi Winery
Bishop's Peak
Caliza Winery
Carina Cellars
Cass Winery
Castoro Cellars
Changala Winery
Chateau Margene
Christian Lazo Wines
Chronic Cellars Winery Inc.
Clavo Cellars
Clayhouse Wines

Croad Vineyards
Cypher Winery
DAOU Vineyards
Dark Star Cellars
Derby Wine Estates
Doce Robles Winery
Donatoni Winery
Eos Estate Winery
Fratelli Perata
Frolicking Frog
FS Cellars
Gelfand Vineyards
Graveyard Vineyards
Grey Wolf Vineyards & Cellars
Harmony Cellars
Hearst Ranch Winery
Hidden Oak Winery
Hunt Cellars
J&J Cellars
J. Lohr Vineyards & Wines
Kenneth Volk Vineyards
Le Vigne Winery
Locatelli Vineyards & Winery
Loma Linda Vineyards LLC
Lone Madrone
Maloy O'Neill Vineyards
Meridian Vineyards
Midnight Cellars
Minassian-Young Vineyards
Mitchella Vineyard & Winery

Moonstone Cellars
Nadeau Family Vintners
Niner Wine Estates
Norman Vineyards
Opolo Vineyards
Ortman Family Wines
Oso Libre Winery
Poalillo Vineyards
Parrish Family Vineyard
PasoPort Wine Company Inc.
Peachy Canyon Winery
Penman Springs Vineyard
Per Cazo Cellars
Pianetta Winery
Pipestone Vineyards
Proulx
Rabbit Ridge Winery
Ranchita Canyon Vineyard
Rangeland Wines
Red Soles Winery
Riverstar Vineyards
Robert Hall Winery
Rocky Creek Cellars
San Marcos Creek Vineyard
Sarzotti Winery
Sculpterra Winery
Silver Horse Winery
Steinbeck Vineyards & Winery
Still Waters Vineyards
Tobin James Cellars

Turley Wine Cellars
Venteux Vineyards
Victor Hugo Winery
Villa San Juliette
Vina Robles
Vines on the Marycrest
Zenaida Cellars

Picpoul Blanc
Lone Madrone
Tablas Creek Vineyard
Terry Hoage Vineyards

Pinot Blanc
Castoro Cellars
Eos Estate Winery

Pinot Grigio
Bianchi Winery
Castoro Cellars
Eberle Winery
Le Vigne Winery
Locatelli Vineyards & Winery
Maloy O'Neill Vineyards
Meridian Vineyards
Moonstone Cellars
Nadeau Family Vintners
Nichols Winery & Cellars
Norman Vineyards

Opolo Vineyards
Orchid Hill Vineyard
Sculpterra Winery
Stephen's Cellar
Still Waters Vineyards

Pinot Gris
Derby Wine Estates
Harmony Cellars
J Dusi Wines
Locatelli Vineyards & Winery
Maloy O'Neill Vineyards
Meridian Vineyards
Nichols Winery & Cellars
Still Waters Vineyards

Pinot Noir
Asuncion Ridge
Adelaida Cellars
Anglim Winery
Barrel 27 Wine Company
Bianchi Winery
Bishop's Peak
Calcareous Vineyard
Carmody McKnight Estate Wines
Castoro Cellars
Cayucos Cellars
Cerro Prieto Vineyard and Cellars
Chateau Margene
Derby Wine Estates

FS Cellars
GreMarK Vineyards
Harmony Cellars
Hearthstone Vineyard & Winery
Hug Cellars
J. Lohr Vineyards & Wines
Jack Creek Cellars
Kenneth Volk Vineyards
Le Vigne Winery
Maloy O'Neill Vineyards
Meridian Vineyards
Midnight Cellars
Nichols Winery & Cellars
Norman Vineyards
Opolo Vineyards
Orchid Hill Vineyard
Ortman Family Wines
Parrish Family Vineyard
Pithy Little Wine Company
Pomar Junction Vineyard & Winery
Rabbit Ridge Winery
Ranchita Canyon Vineyard
Sculpterra Winery
Sextant Wines
STANGER
Stephen's Cellar
Tassajara Cellars
Tobin James Cellars
Twilight Cellars
Venteux Vineyards

Wild Horse Winery & Vineyards
Windward Vineyard

Port
Anglim Winery
Arroyo Robles Winery
Cass Winery
Castoro Cellars
Cayucos Cellars
Chronic Cellars Winery Inc.
Chumeia Vineyards
Cinquain Cellars
Clautiere Vineyard
Clayhouse Wines
Cypher Winery
D'Anbino Vineyards & Cellars
Dark Star Cellars
Derby Wine Estates
Dover Canyon Winery
Eberle Winery
Eos Estate Winery
Graveyard Vineyards
GreMarK Vineyards
Halter Ranch Vineyard
Harmony Cellars
Hunt Cellars
J Dusi Wines
J&J Cellars
JUSTIN Vineyards & Winery
Le Vigne Winery

Maloy O'Neill Vineyards
Midnight Cellars
Minassian-Young Vineyards
Mitchella Vineyard & Winery
Opolo Vineyards
PasoPort Wine Company Inc.
Peachy Canyon Winery
Pear Valley Vineyard
Penman Springs Vineyard
Pipestone Vineyards
Ranchita Canyon Vineyard
Riverstar Vineyards
RN Estate Vineyard & Winery
Robert Hall Winery
Rotta Winery
Roxo Port Cellars
Summerwood Winery
Twilight Cellars
Veris Cellars
Wild Coyote Estate Winery

Primitivo

AronHill Vineyards
August Ridge Vineyards
Caliza Winery
Castoro Cellars
Loma Linda Vineyards LLC
Maloy O'Neill Vineyards
Sextant Wines
Tobin James Cellars
Zenaida Cellars

Red Rhône Blend

Asuncion Ridge
Adelaida Cellars
Alta Colina Vineyard & Winery
AmByth Estate
Ancient Peaks Winery
Anglim Winery
Arroyo Robles Winery
Booker Vineyard
Calcareous Vineyard
Caliza Winery
Carina Cellars
Cass Winery
Changala Winery
Chateau Margene
Chronic Cellars Winery Inc.
Cinquain Cellars
Clautiere Vineyard
Clayhouse Wines
Croad Vineyards
Cypher Winery
DAOU Vineyards
Dark Star Cellars
Denner Vineyards
Derby Wine Estates
Dover Canyon Winery
Eberle Winery
Ecluse Wines
Edward Sellers Vineyards & Wines
Epoch Estate Wines
Halter Ranch Vineyard
Hearst Ranch Winery

Hearthstone Vineyard & Winery
Herman Story Wines
Hug Cellars
Hunt Cellars
J. Lohr Vineyards & Wines
Jacob Toft
Jada Vineyard & Winery
JK Wine Company
JUSTIN Vineyards & Winery
Kaleidos
Kiamie Wine Cellars
Kukkula
L'Aventure Winery
Le Vigne Winery
Linne Calodo Cellars
Lone Madrone
Maloy O'Neill Vineyards
Minassian-Young Vineyards
Mitchella Vineyard & Winery
Mondo Cellars
Nadeau Family Vintners
Opolo Vineyards
Ortman Family Wines
Oso Libre Winery
Parrish Family Vineyard
Peachy Canyon Winery
Pear Valley Vineyard
Per Cazo Cellars
Pipestone Vineyards
Per Cazo Cellars
Pipestone Vineyards
Proulx
Rabbit Ridge Winery

Ranchita Canyon Vineyard
Riverstar Vineyards
RN Estate Vineyard & Winery
Robert Hall Winery
Sculpterra Winery
Sextant Wines
Stacked Stone Cellars
Summerwood Winery
Tablas Creek Vineyard
Terry Hoage Vineyards
Thacher Winery
Tolo Cellars
Treana and Hope Family Wines
Twilight Cellars
Venteux Vineyards
Villa Creek Cellars
Villicana Winery
Vina Robles
Vines on the Marycrest
Westberg Cellars
Zenaida Cellars

Refosco
Bianchi Winery
Tobin James Cellars

Riesling
Bishop's Peak
Chronic Cellars Winery Inc.
Harmony Cellars
J. Lohr Vineyards & Wines
Meridian Vineyards

Rosé
Ancient Peaks Winery
Anglim Winery
Arroyo Robles Winery
B & E Vineyard/Winery
Barrel 27 Wine Company
Bella Luna Winery
Calcareous Vineyard
Caliza Winery
Cass Winery
Clautiere Vineyard
Clavo Cellars
Clayhouse Wines
Cypher Winery
D'Anbino Vineyards & Cellars
Eberle Winery
Edward Sellers Vineyards & Wines
Eos Estate Winery
Frolicking Frog
Gelfand Vineyards
Graveyard Vineyards
GreMarK Vineyards
Grey Wolf Vineyards & Cellars
Halter Ranch Vineyard
HammerSky Vineyards
Hearst Ranch Winery
Hug Cellars
Hunt Cellars
J&J Cellars
J. Lohr Vineyards & Wines
L'Aventure Winery
Le Cuvier

Le Vigne Winery
Loma Linda Vineyards LLC
Midnight Cellars
Mitchella Vineyard & Winery
Niner Wine Estates
Ortman Family Wines
Oso Libre Winery
Penman Springs Vineyard
Pianetta Winery
Pipestone Vineyards
Pithy Little Wine Company
Pomar Junction Vineyard & Winery
Rabbit Ridge Winery
Ranchita Canyon Vineyard
Rangeland Wines
Red Soles Winery
Robert Hall Winery
Rockin' R Winery
Rotta Winery
Sextant Wines
Starr Ranch Vineyards and Winery
Still Waters Vineyards
Tablas Creek Vineyard
Terry Hoage Vineyards
Thacher Winery
Tobin James Cellars
Twilight Cellars
Victor Hugo Winery
Villa Creek Cellars
Villicana Winery
Vines on the Marycrest
Wild Coyote Estate Winery
Wild Horse Winery & Vineyards

Roussanne

Adelaida Cellars
Alta Colina Vineyard & Winery
AmByth Estate
Anglim Winery
Barrel 27 Wine Company
Caliza Winery
Cass Winery
Chronic Cellars Winery Inc.
Clautiere Vineyard
Dover Canyon Winery
Edward Sellers Vineyards & Wines
Eos Estate Winery
Grey Wolf Vineyards & Cellars
Hearthstone Vineyard & Winery
JK Wine Company
Kenneth Volk Vineyards
L'Aventure Winery
Lone Madrone
Mitchella Vineyard & Winery
Nichols Winery & Cellars
Opolo Vineyards
Per Cazo Cellars
Pipestone Vineyards
Proulx
Summerwood Winery
Tablas Creek Vineyard
Terry Hoage Vineyards
Twilight Cellars
Venteux Vineyards
Villa Creek Cellars

Sangiovese

AJB Vineyards
AmByth Estate
August Ridge Vineyards
Bella Luna Winery
Berardo Vineyards and Winery
Bianchi Winery
Caparone Winery
Chateau Margene
Doce Robles Winery
Donatoni Winery
Dover Canyon Winery
Eberle Winery
Eos Estate Winery
Fratelli Perata
Hunt Cellars
Laraneta Winery
Le Cuvier
Le Vigne Winery
Maloy O'Neill Vineyards
Meridian Vineyards
Midnight Cellars
Moonstone Cellars
Niner Wine Estates
Opolo Vineyards
Orchid Hill Vineyard
Ortman Family Wines
Peachy Canyon Winery
Pianetta Winery
Pithy Little Wine Company
Ranchita Canyon Vineyard
Tobin James Cellars

Sauvignon Blanc

Ancient Peaks Winery
August Ridge Vineyards
Bianchi Winery
Bishop's Peak
Cerro Prieto Vineyard and Cellars
Cinquain Cellars
Clavo Cellars
Clayhouse Wines
D'Anbino Vineyards & Cellars
Eberle Winery
Eos Estate Winery
Frolicking Frog
GreMarK Vineyards
Halter Ranch Vineyard
Hearst Ranch Winery
Hidden Oak Winery
Hug Cellars
Hunt Cellars
J&J Cellars
J. Lohr Vineyards & Wines
JUSTIN Vineyards & Winery
Le Vigne Winery
Locatelli Vineyards & Winery
Maloy O'Neill Vineyards
Meridian Vineyards
Mitchella Vineyard & Winery
Moonstone Cellars
Niner Wine Estates
Parrish Family Vineyard
Pithy Little Wine Company
Pretty-Smith Vineyards & Winery

Ranchita Canyon Vineyard
Riverstar Vineyards
RN Estate Vineyard & Winery
Robert Hall Winery
San Marcos Creek Vineyard
Sculpterra Winery
Still Waters Vineyards
Veris Cellars
Villa San Juliette
Vina Robles

Sparkling Wines
Arroyo Robles Winery
Bianchi Winery
Carmody McKnight Estate Wines
Cass Winery
Derby Wine Estates
J&J Cellars
Le Vigne Winery
Veris Cellars

Syrah
Adelaida Cellars
AJB Vineyards
Alta Colina Vineyard & Winery
AmByth Estate
Anglim Winery
Arroyo Robles Winery
B & E Vineyard/Winery
Bear Cave Cellars
Barrel 27 Wine Company
Berardo Vineyards and Winery

Bianchi Winery
Bishop's Peak
Brochelle Vineyards
Calcareous Vineyard
Caliza Winery
Carina Cellars
Cass Winery
Castoro Cellars
Cayucos Cellars
Cerro Prieto Vineyard and Cellars
Changala Winery
Chronic Cellars Winery Inc.
Chumeia Vineyards
Cinquain Cellars
Clautiere Vineyard
Clavo Cellars
Clayhouse Wines
Croad Vineyards
Cypher Winery
D'Anbino Vineyards & Cellars
DAOU Vineyards
Denner Vineyards
Derby Wine Estates
Doce Robles Winery
Donatoni Winery
Dover Canyon Winery
Dunning Vineyards Estate Winery
Eberle Winery
Ecluse Wines
Edward Sellers Vineyards & Wines
Eos Estate Winery
Falcon Nest Winery

Four Sisters Ranch
Frolicking Frog
Gelfand Vineyards
Graveyard Vineyards
Grey Wolf Vineyards & Cellars
Halter Ranch Vineyard
Hansen Winery
Harmony Cellars
Hearthstone Vineyard & Winery
Herman Story Wines
Hug Cellars
Hunt Cellars
J Dusi Wines
J. Lohr Vineyards & Wines
Jack Creek Cellars
Jada Vineyard & Winery
JK Wine Company
JUSTIN Vineyards & Winery
Kaleidos
Kenneth Volk Vineyards
L'Aventure Winery
Le Cuvier
Le Vigne Winery
Linne Calodo Cellars
Lone Madrone
Madison Cellars
Maloy O'Neill Vineyards
Meridian Vineyards
Midnight Cellars
Minassian-Young Vineyards
Mitchella Vineyard & Winery
Moonstone Cellars
Nadeau Family Vintners

Nichols Winery & Cellars
Niner Wine Estates
Opolo Vineyards
Orchid Hill Vineyard
Ortman Family Wines
Oso Libre Winery
Pear Valley Vineyard
Penman Springs Vineyard
Per Cazo Cellars
Pianetta Winery
Pipestone Vineyards
Pithy Little Wine Company
Pomar Junction Vineyard & Winery
Proulx
Rangeland Wines
Red Soles Winery
Riverstar Vineyards
RN Estate Vineyard & Winery
Rabbit Ridge Winery
Robert Hall Winery
Rocky Creek Cellars
San Marcos Creek Vineyard
Sarzotti Winery
Sculpterra Winery
Sextant Wines
STANGER
Starr Ranch Vineyards and Winery
Still Waters Vineyards
Summerwood Winery
Tablas Creek Vineyard
Tassajara Cellars
Terry Hoage Vineyards
Thacher Winery

Tobin James Cellars
Tolo Cellars
Treana and Hope Family Wines
Twilight Cellars
Venteux Vineyards
Veris Cellars
Via Vega Winery
Victor Hugo Winery
Villa Creek Cellars
Villicana Winery
Vina Robles
Vines on the Marycrest
Wild Coyote Estate Winery
Wild Horse Winery & Vineyards
Zenaida Cellars

Tannat
Arroyo Robles Winery
Chronic Cellars Winery Inc.
Clayhouse Wines
HammerSky Vineyards
Le Vigne Winery
Lone Madrone
Tablas Creek Vineyard

Tempranillo
AmByth Estate
Arroyo Robles Winery
Barrel 27 Wine Company
Bella Luna Winery
Bodegas M
Bodegas Paso Robles

Booker Vineyard
Caliza Winery
Castoro Cellars
Chronic Cellars Winery Inc.
Clayhouse Wines
Cypher Winery
Edward Sellers Vineyards & Wines
Eos Estate Winery
Epoch Estate Wines
Grey Wolf Vineyards & Cellars
Hearst Ranch Winery
J&J Cellars
JUSTIN Vineyards & Winery
Kenneth Volk Vineyards
Maloy O'Neill Vineyards
Minassian-Young Vineyards
Mitchella Vineyard & Winery
Opolo Vineyards
PasoPort Wine Company Inc.
Red Soles Winery
Silver Horse Winery
STANGER
Starr Ranch Vineyards and Winery
Tobin James Cellars
Villa Creek Cellars

Verdelho
Kenneth Volk Vineyards
PasoPort Wine Company Inc.
Vina Robles
Wild Horse Winery & Vineyards

Vermentino
Clavo Cellars
Tablas Creek Vineyard

Viognier
Adelaida Cellars
AJB Vineyards
Alta Colina Vineyard & Winery
AmByth Estate
Anglim Winery
Arroyo Robles Winery
Barrel 27 Wine Company
Berardo Vineyards and Winery
Calcareous Vineyard
Caliza Winery
Carina Cellars
Cass Winery
Changala Winery
Chronic Cellars Winery Inc.
Chumeia Vineyards
Clautiere Vineyard
Clavo Cellars
Croad Vineyards
DAOU Vineyards
Denner Vineyards
Doce Robles Winery
Dover Canyon Winery
Edward Sellers Vineyards & Wines
Eos Estate Winery
Frolicking Frog
GreMarK Vineyards
Grey Wolf Vineyards & Cellars

Halter Ranch Vineyard
Hansen Winery
Hidden Oak Winery
Hug Cellars
J&J Cellars
J. Lohr Vineyards & Wines
JK Wine Company
JUSTIN Vineyards & Winery
Kenneth Volk Vineyards
Le Vigne Winery
Linne Calodo Cellars
Lone Madrone
Madison Cellars
Mitchella Vineyard & Winery
Moonstone Cellars
Nichols Winery & Cellars
Opolo Vineyards
Orchid Hill Vineyard
Oso Libre Winery
Peachy Canyon Winery
Pipestone Vineyards
Pithy Little Wine Company
Poalillo Vineyards
Pomar Junction Vineyard & Winery
Pozo Valley
Proulx
Red Soles Winery
Robert Hall Winery
STANGER
Steinbeck Vineyards & Winery
Still Waters Vineyards
Summerwood Winery
Tablas Creek Vineyard

Thacher Winery
Twilight Cellars
Venteux Vineyards
Veris Cellars
Victor Hugo Winery
Villicana Winery
Vina Robles
Wild Horse Winery & Vineyards
Zenaida Cellars

White Blend
Adelaida Cellars
Alta Colina Vineyard & Winery
AmByth Estate
Ancient Peaks Winery
Anglim Winery
AronHill Vineyards
Booker Vineyard
Calcareous Vineyard
Caliza Winery
Cass Winery
Castoro Cellars
Changala Winery
Chronic Cellars Winery Inc.
Chumeia Vineyards
Cinquain Cellars
Clayhouse Wines
DAOU Vineyards
Denner Vineyards
Derby Wine Estates
Dover Canyon Winery
Ecluse Wines

Edward Sellers Vineyards & Wines
Eos Estate Winery
Graveyard Vineyards
Grey Wolf Vineyards & Cellars
Halter Ranch Vineyard
Hearst Ranch Winery
Hearthstone Vineyard & Winery
Herman Story Wines
Hunt Cellars
J. Lohr Vineyards & Wines
Jacob Toft
Jada Vineyard & Winery
JK Wine Company
Kaleidos
Kenneth Volk Vineyards
Kiamie Wine Cellars
Kukkula
La FÃªte
Lone Madrone
Midnight Cellars
Minassian-Young Vineyards
Mitchella Vineyard & Winery
Mondo Cellars
Moonstone Cellars
Nadeau Family Vintners
Per Cazo Cellars
Riverstar Vineyards
Robert Hall Winery
Rockin' R Winery
San Marcos Creek Vineyard
Sextant Wines
Still Waters Vineyards
Summerwood Winery

Tablas Creek Vineyard
Terry Hoage Vineyards
Treana and Hope Family Wines
Turley Wine Cellars
Venteux Vineyards
Veris Cellars
Villa Creek Cellars
Vina Robles
Westberg Cellars
Zenaida Cellars

White Zinfandel
Castoro Cellars
J. Lohr Vineyards & Wines

Zinfandel
Adelaida Cellars
AJB Vineyards
Ancient Peaks Winery
Anglim Winery
Arroyo Robles Winery
Bear Cave Cellars
Bella Luna Winery
Berardo Vineyards and Winery
Bianchi Winery
Brochelle Vineyards
Calcareous Vineyard
Caparone Winery
Carina Cellars
Castoro Cellars
Cayucos Cellars
Changala Winery

Chateau Margene
Christian Lazo Wines
Chronic Cellars Winery Inc.
Chumeia Vineyards
Clavo Cellars
Clayhouse Wines
Croad Vineyards
CrossLynn Estate
Cypher Winery
DAOU Vineyards
Dark Star Cellars
Derby Wine Estates
Doce Robles Winery
Donatoni Winery
Dover Canyon Winery
Dunning Vineyards Estate Winery
Eberle Winery
Ecluse Wines
Edward Sellers Vineyards & Wines
Eos Estate Winery
Epoch Estate Wines
Falcon Nest Winery
Fratelli Perata
Frolicking Frog
FS Cellars
Gelfand Vineyards
Graveyard Vineyards
GreMarK Vineyards
Grey Wolf Vineyards & Cellars
HammerSky Vineyards
Hansen Winery
Harmony Cellars

Hearthstone Vineyard & Winery
Hug Cellars
Hunt Cellars
J Dusi
J&J Cellars
J. Lohr Vineyards & Wines
JUSTIN Vineyards & Winery
Kenneth Volk Vineyards
Le Cuvier
Le Vigne Winery
Linne Calodo Cellars
Locatelli Vineyards & Winery
Loma Linda Vineyards LLC
Lone Madrone
Maloy O'Neill Vineyards
Meridian Vineyards
Midnight Cellars
Minassian-Young Vineyards
Mitchella Vineyard & Winery
Mondo Cellars
Moonstone Cellars
Nadeau Family Vintners
Nichols Winery & Cellars
Norman Vineyards
Opolo Vineyards
Orchid Hill Vineyard
Oso Libre Winery
Parrish Family Vineyard
PasoPort Wine Company Inc.
Peachy Canyon Winery
Pear Valley Vineyard
Per Cazo Cellars
Pianetta Winery

Pipestone Vineyards
Pithy Little Wine Company
Poalillo Vineyards
Pomar Junction Vineyard & Winery
Pozo Valley
Proulx
Rabbit Ridge Winery
Ranchita Canyon Vineyard
Rangeland Wines
Red Soles Winery
Riverstar Vineyards
Rocky Creek Cellars
Rotta Winery
San Marcos Creek Vineyard
Sarzotti Winery
Sculpterra Winery
Sextant Wines
Stacked Stone Cellars
Steinbeck Vineyards & Winery
Still Waters Vineyards
Tackitt Family Vineyards
Thacher Winery
Tobin James Cellars
Tolo Cellars
Treana and Hope Family Wines
Turley Wine Cellars
Twilight Cellars
Veris Cellars
Via Vega Winery
Victor Hugo Winery
Villa San Juliette
Villicana Winery
Vina Robles

Vines on the Marycrest
RN Estate Vineyard & Winery
Vista Del Rey Vineyards
Westberg Cellars
Wild Coyote Estate Winery
Wild Horse Winery & Vineyards
Zenaida Cellars
Zin Alley

The wineries of Paso Robles continue to deliver fabulous wines. Each vintage seems to be better than the last with more talented winemakers moving to the area each year.

Plan a wine trip to Paso Robles soon and discover a new wine and perhaps make a few new friends.

For additional food and wine information
visit eatthiswith.com